NEAB /AQA

Working with the English
Anthology
2000/2001

Imelda Pilgrim
Lindsay McNab
Paul Osman

Alemao

Contents

Introduction

This book is intended to provide you with support and practice as you study the poems in the **Anthology** for NEAB GCSE English.

The full text of each poem is presented alongside stimulating photographs and activities. You will find short poems, long poems, humorous poems and angry poems. Some are focused on places, many are about people and ways of living. We strongly recommend that you talk about the poems and read them aloud. This will provide an excellent way of gaining a better understanding of the poems as you prepare to write about them.

In Part 1 of Paper 2, Poets in the English Literary Heritage, you will be expected to write about one of the poets: either Simon Armitage, Carol Ann Duffy or Ted Hughes. In Part 2 of Paper 2, Poems from Other Cultures and Traditions, you will be required to write about a selection of the poems.

To help you prepare for the examination this book provides:

- **an introduction to each poet in the English Literary Heritage** including thoughts about poetry and their poems from Simon Armitage, Carol Ann Duffy and Ted Hughes

- **background information for the Poems from Other Cultures and Traditions** including biographical notes on the poets and explanations of concepts which may be unfamiliar

- **activities to explore each poem and the poems together, focusing on the key assessment objectives of interpretation, structure and language** to help you focus your ideas and build your response on what the examiner is looking for. The assessment objectives are clearly explained in the section on the poems together, and a checklist of assessment objectives is presented with each poem

- **writing assignments** which provide opportunities for an extended written response to a poem or group of poems, along with related original writing assignments

- **practice questions and model answer plans** giving plenty of practice and detailed suggestions on how to approach a question, what the examiner is looking for and how to structure your answer to show your understanding

- **guidance on preparing for the examination and a glossary** for useful reference.

We hope that you enjoy your course and the poems in this selection. Ted Hughes feels that a poem should be read differently from the way a postcard from a friend or an instruction manual might be read. Poetry needs a special kind of reading. We hope that the activities in this book will help you find that special kind of reading and make the poems come alive for you.

1 Simon Armitage

Simon Armitage was born and brought up in West Yorkshire. After taking a degree in Geography at Portsmouth, he qualified as a social worker and spent the next six years working for the probation service. He is now a freelance writer and television and radio broadcaster. Simon Armitage has this to say about how he started writing poetry and why he still writes now:

'I started writing poetry because I was homesick. I was away at college and I started reading Ted Hughes's book, *The Remains of Elmet*, which has lots of photographs of West Yorkshire, where I come from. We'd studied him at school and I was trying to reconnect to that. So it was a sense of loss that got me writing. The reason that I keep on writing is to do with making a connection with the world, a connection which I see becoming more and more distant; it's a connection which gets harder to find. I think when I first read Ted Hughes's poems they made me realize that you can describe that feeling through images. Poetry with a single voice where somebody believes very firmly in what they're saying, can be very powerful. We usually expect power to come with noise and chrome and technicolour, but poetry is a very simple matter; it's just a pen on a piece of paper, something incredibly intimate, just little marks in black on a piece of white...'

Poetry and the business of writing and reading poetry is seen by Simon Armitage as a 'system of thought'. He believes firmly in 'the right of poetry to ask questions..., to set up an issue for thought and consideration' and he also believes that he does not 'own' the way the poems should be read, or how we interpret them:

'A lot of my poems are about feelings, so one way of approaching a poem is to read it, see how it makes you feel and then try and say why. You could start by comparing it to something you are already familiar with. You can look things up in a dictionary and wonder about particular lines. Poetry is a very compact language, so you can think about whether there is another meaning to some of the words; it can be like looking into a pond – will something else come into focus? One thing you shouldn't do is assume there's some kind of key that will "turn" this poem, or that there's some code that you've got to press.'

When asked whether his poems are autobiographical, Simon Armitage makes the point that 'most poetry has to come from personal experience of one kind or another'. For example, the **untitled poem** is autobiographical in the sense that it is based on his memories of school:

'I think about what the person did in the same way that I think about bullies who do brutal and violent things; because they are looking for attention, they have to do it in front of other people. There's a line in the poem which says "don't believe me, please, if I say", but really, you've got to believe me, otherwise why would I be bothering to write a poem? This is a bit like the first line in the poem. It's possible to read this line, with its slightly sarcastic tone, as saying I'm not really bothered at all, but I want the reader to see the tone of these opening lines as a lie which covers up the real feelings. The poem is the same length as a sonnet (a traditional form, usually associated with love poetry) and you could say that it attempts to make fun of the sonnet form, but fails because it is, essentially, a poem about two people and how one tries to grab hold of another.'

Poem also follows the rules of the sonnet form. Some people criticize the poem for not coming up with a conclusion about what this man did; others see the poem as a legitimate summary of the man's life. Simon Armitage asks: 'How can you judge this person? Here's somebody who for three-quarters of his life, or for three lines in every quatrain, did something good and then he did something bad and in one case, something that would be seen as unforgivable; so how do we judge him in the end? I'm declaring the right not to answer the question, just to ask it.'

It Ain't What You Do It's What It Does To You makes the point that people don't have to travel or have wild experiences in order to have something to write about:

'Black Moss is a very lonely place, on the border between Yorkshire and Lancashire. It's on top of a hill and all you can see is the sky and the water. The boy at the day centre was a part of my work. Through looking closely at detail, you can go on to elaborate about the world, the universe, the cosmos. This poem is about the sheer enjoyment of being alive.'

'**Cataract Operation** is a poem which sets up a series of images. It's almost as if the first image has occasioned the rest. When I wrote it I was probably thinking of some contemporary poets who were renowned for their brilliant images – like calling a lightbulb an electric pear, for example. I was very impressed with that kind of writing, but you can be critical of it too. Where does it take us? What does it mean? Is it cleverness or is it just showing off? I do think that imagery is the cornerstone of writing, but I'm trying to take it one step further in this poem and say that you can bedazzle yourself to the point where you stop seeing the world, and poetry for me is a way of seeing the world. It's a way of making sense of the world and connecting with it. That's why, in the end, I "drop the blind" (line 15); I stop being silly; I stop showing off. The message is that if I stop blinding myself with these ridiculous images, I can go back to writing the poems I really want to write.'

Both **Cataract Operation** and **About His Person** show Simon Armitage's interest in expressions we use as part of everyday language. The title of **About His Person** is a phrase used by police when listing the possessions found on a person whose death may become the subject of an inquiry. He comments that the poem is 'entirely substantiated with puns; nearly every word has a double meaning... Part of the point of the poem is that we are constructing somebody from the things which they carried with them'.

I am very bothered when I think
of the bad things I have done in my life.
Not least that time in the chemistry lab
when I held a pair of scissors by the blades
5 and played the handles
in the naked lilac flame of the Bunsen burner;
then called your name, and handed them over.

O the unrivalled stench of branded skin
as you slipped your thumb and middle finger in,
10 then couldn't shake off the two burning rings. Marked,
the doctor said, for eternity.

Don't believe me, please, if I say
that was just my butterfingered way, at thirteen,
of asking you if you would marry me.

Explanations

This poem is taken from a collection of untitled poems called **A Book of Matches**. Each poem was designed to be read in the time it takes for a match to burn down. The main incident described here had its origins in a school joke: you never took a set of lab tongs if they were offered to you. The poet found the first two lines in a probation service questionnaire.

O the unrivalled: This part of line 8 hints at romantic, pre-twentieth-century love poetry

branded: burned with an identifying mark to indicate ownership. Nowadays we talk about 'brand names' of products

butterfingered: unable to hold things, clumsy: butter was also once used to treat burns

Exploring the poem

(1) The poem recalls an incident at school. What is happening in each section? Match the line numbers to the most appropriate description.

- lines 1–2   **a** making a comparison
- lines 3–7   **b** explaining feelings
- lines 8–11   **c** explaining how the person in the poem feels now
- lines 12–14   **d** explaining what happened

(2) The poem is written in the first person. Who do you think this person is addressing? Give your reasons.

(3) Is there evidence to suggest that the girl and boy liked each other?

Language

(4) The last stanza (see glossary, page 95) suggests that the incident described was a kind of marriage proposal. Pick out the words in stanza two which establish this metaphor (see glossary, page 93). Explain why you chose them.

(5) What is suggested by the use of the word 'butterfingered' in line 13?

Structure

(6) The way the poem is structured gives more clues about feelings.

- In stanza one the rhyming words 'name' and 'flame' are positioned underneath each other. Why do you think the poet has done this?
- Look at the words 'Marked' in stanza two and 'at thirteen' in stanza three. How does the poet make these words stand out? Why might he want to highlight them?

(7) The first lines of each stanza raise questions about how seriously we should take the poem.

- What is the effect of the contrast between the words 'O the unrivalled…' and 'stench of branded skin' (line 8)?
- Think about lines 1 and 12. What different meanings could they have? How should they be read aloud?

Writing

1 Is this a love poem? Consider what each stanza reveals of the person's thoughts and feelings.

2 Write about something you did in the past that you now regret. Think about:
- how you thought or felt about it at the time
- how you feel or think about it now.

Poem

And if it snowed and snow covered the drive
he took a spade and tossed it to one side.
And always tucked his daughter up at night.
And slippered her the one time that she lied.

5   And every week he tipped up half his wage.
And what he didn't spend each week he saved.
And praised his wife for every meal she made.
And once, for laughing, punched her in the face.

And for his mum he hired a private nurse.
10 And every Sunday taxied her to church.
And he blubbed when she went from bad to worse.
And twice he lifted ten quid from her purse.

Here's how they rated him when they looked back:
sometimes he did this, sometimes he did that.

Explanations

slippered: hit with a slipper
tipped up: handed over
blubbed: a shortened version of
'blubbered', meaning to cry
uncontrollably

Exploring the poem

1. **Poem** gives eleven different examples of things the man did. List the examples under the headings **Good** and **Bad**. Are there any which could be described as both? Explain why.

2. Which of the following adjectives best describe the man? Give reasons.

   - violent
   - responsible
   - domineering
   - caring
   - jealous
   - energetic
   - tight-fisted
   - conventional
   - considerate
   - conscientious
   - boring
   - reliable

   What other words would you use to describe this man?

3. Who do you think 'they' (line 13) are?
   - Which lines in each stanza (see glossary, page 95) might 'they' have said?
   - Who gives the information for the other lines?

   How successful do you find this pattern?

4. What occasion might the poem be written for?

Structure

5. How do the following features of the poem help to reinforce an impression of the man:
   - the rhythm (see glossary, page 95)   • the repetition of the word 'And'?

6. How does the fourth line in each of the first three stanzas affect the way you read the lines which come before it?

7. Look carefully at the definition of sonnet in the glossary (page 95). How perfect is **Poem** as an example of the sonnet form?

8. How 'perfect' was the life led by the man in the poem?

Language

9. This is a very 'plain' and simply written poem. For example, there are no metaphors (see glossary, page 93) and very few words of more than one syllable (see glossary, page 95). Why do you think the poet chose to write the poem in this way?

10. The title of this poem is unusual. How much 'poetry' do you think this man had in his life?

Writing

1. Is the poem:
   - sad   • serious   • humorous   • sarcastic   • neutral?

   What does the tone or mood (see glossary, pages 94, 95) of the poem suggest about the poet's intention?

2. To what extent do the structure and language of **Poem** reflect the man's life?

3. Does **Poem** give you ideas about how you want to live your life? What would you like people to say about you?

   Write a poem based on the way you live your life. You could use the sonnet form, or any other poetic form.

It Ain't What You Do
It's What It Does To You

I have not bummed across America
with only a dollar to spare, one pair
of busted Levi's and a bowie knife.
I have lived with thieves in Manchester.

5   I have not padded through the Taj Mahal,
barefoot, listening to the space between
each footfall picking up and putting down
its print against the marble floor. But I

skimmed flat stones across Black Moss on a day
10 so still I could hear each set of ripples
as they crossed. I felt each stone's inertia
spend itself against the water; then sink.

I have not toyed with a parachute cord
while perched on the lip of a light-aircraft;
15 but I held the wobbly head of a boy
at the day centre, and stroked his fat hands.

And I guess that the tightness in the throat
and the tiny cascading sensation
somewhere inside us are both part of that
20 sense of something else. That feeling, I mean.

Explanations

**It Ain't What You Do It's What It Does
To You:** a play on the words of an old
popular song: 'It ain't what you do it's
the way that you do it'
bummed: hitchhiked and slept rough
bowie knife: a large sheath knife with a
pointed blade
Taj Mahal: a marble tomb of great
splendour and beauty in Agra, India
Black Moss: a shallow and isolated
moorland lake on the border between
Lancashire and Yorkshire
inertia: the heavy, motionless state of
matter before an outside force acts on it
cascading: a rushing of water, or the
tumbling of a waterfall

Exploring the poem

1. What sort of things and experiences does the poet value? Choose from the words below and find evidence in the poem to support your choices:

   - quietness
   - stillness
   - solitude
   - adventure
   - people
   - places
   - journeys
   - feelings

Structure

2. At first it appears that the poet is emphasizing the differences between other people's experiences and his own. The words 'I have not' are very assertive. But if you look closely at the structure of the poem you will see that he is exploring the similarities. He uses the words 'I have not' to divide the poem into a series of comparisons, both within and between stanzas (see glossary, page 95).

   List the comparisons the poet makes. Explain the point he is making with each.

Language

3. Sound patterns (see glossary, page 95) help the poet to share some of his feelings and experiences. Look closely at stanza three:
   - The sound of the word 'skimmed' helps to give an impression of what it describes (see onomatopoeia in the glossary, page 94). What does this word suggest to you?
   - When a flat stone is skimmed across the water it bounces. The vowel sounds (see glossary, page 95) in lines 11 and 12 help to suggest the time lapses between each bounce; for example, 'each' has a short vowel sound and 'stones' has a long vowel sound.

   Choose three more words from these lines and show how they might suggest the different time lapses.

4. The poet uses imagery (see glossary, page 93) to make connections between different experiences. Look closely at stanza four.
   - What feelings are suggested by the image in the first two lines?
   - What feelings are suggested by the image in the last two lines?

5. Look at stanza five. What kinds of feelings are described here? In what ways could lines 13–14 be read as a metaphor (see glossary, page 93) which compares these feelings with the experience of parachuting from a light aircraft?

Writing

1. To what extent is this poem about experiences and feelings? Give reasons for your answer.

2. In stanza three the poet writes about circles of ripples which cross over each other. Notice that these lines are placed at the centre of the poem. How might this image reflect the ideas and feelings of the poem as a whole?

Cataract Operation

The sun comes like a head
through last night's turtleneck.

A pigeon in the yard turns tail
and offers me a card. Any card.

5   From pillar to post, a pantomime
of damp, forgotten washing

on the washing line.
So, in the breeze:

the olé of a crimson towel,
10   the cancan of a ra ra skirt,

the monkey business of a shirt
pegged only by its sleeve,

the cheerio
of a handkerchief.

15   I drop the blind
but not before a company

of half a dozen hens
struts through the gate,

looks round the courtyard
20   for a contact lens.

Explanations

cataract: 1 the lens of the eye becomes cloudy, leading eventually to blindness **2** a large waterfall

operation: 1 working action **2** movement **3** medical procedure

turtleneck: a high-necked sweater

turns tail: turn your back on something, run away, or 'take flight'

from pillar to post: looking everywhere for something, or going from one resource to another

pantomime: an entertainment usually based on a fairy tale, which can include singing, dancing, clowning, acrobatics and a scene in which someone, or something, is transformed

olé: a Spanish word used for applause

cancan: a high-kicking dance

ra ra skirt: a short, frilly skirt worn for parades

monkey business: mischievous behaviour

cheerio: an informal goodbye

handkerchief: handkerchiefs are sometimes used to wave goodbye

company: 1 a group **2** a group of soldiers

strut: to walk in a way which shows off, or suggests your importance

courtyard: space enclosed by walls or buildings

Exploring the poem

1. This poem is a mixture of story and puzzle. Most stories provide answers to the following questions: Who? What? Where? When? Why?

   Look again at the poem and its title and see which of these questions can be answered. Put your answers together to make a story.

2. The poem can be compared to a magic eye picture. If you study it for long enough, the picture changes and hidden images emerge. The following images (see glossary, page 93) are listed in the order they appear in the poem. How many of them can you find and what do they describe?

   a a waterfall   d a conjuring act   g a falcon
   b an amphibious reptile   e a bull fight   h a parade
   c a dove   f an Egyptian sun god   i a circus

3. Which parts of the picture in the poem are real and which parts imagined? List in sequence the things which happen which seem to be real, quoting evidence from the text to support your views, for example:

   Stanza 1 The sun comes out after a wet night.

Language

4. By changing ordinary everyday things into extraordinary images, the poet creates a vivid picture and a sense of movement. He does this through his choice of words, his use of colloquial expressions (see glossary, page 93) and his use of metaphor (see glossary, page 93). Here, for example, is how he describes the pigeon:

   'The expression "turns tail" is particularly effective because it suggests that the pigeon is turning and "taking flight", all in one quick movement. Comparing the tail to a magician fanning out a pack of cards also works well because it expresses the magic of a brief moment when the pigeon opens out its tail feathers.'

   Pick out some other lines which create a similarly colourful picture and explain what they are describing, how they work and how effective you find them.

Structure

5. The poet creates links within and between lines which help the poem to flow, for example the cheerful rhythm (see glossary, page 95) of lines 9–14. Find specific examples of:
   - rhyming sounds (see glossary, page 95)
   - alliteration (see glossary, page 93)
   - links between images.

6. Look again at what the poet says about this poem on page 5.
   - What do you think is meant by 'I drop the blind'?
   - Why do you think the blind is dropped in line 15 and not in the last line?
   - How is the rhythm in the poem changed by this line?

Writing

Explain how each of the statements below describes **Cataract Operation**, using evidence from the poem to support your explanations.
- It tells a story.
- It celebrates ordinary things.
- It's a magic eye picture.
- It's about writing poetry.

About His Person

Five pounds fifty in change, exactly,
a library card on its date of expiry.

A postcard, stamped,
unwritten, but franked,

5   a pocket-size diary slashed with a pencil
from March twenty-fourth to the first of April.

A brace of keys for a mortise lock,
an analogue watch, self-winding, stopped.

A final demand
10 in his own hand,

a rolled-up note of explanation
planted there like a spray carnation

but beheaded, in his fist.
A shopping list.

15 A giveaway photograph stashed in his wallet,
a keepsake banked in the heart of a locket.

No gold or silver,
but crowning one finger

a ring of white unweathered skin.
20 That was everything.

Explanations

About His Person: a reference to the
expression used by police when they itemize
the possessions found on a body
franked: when a letter goes through the post the
stamp is cancelled so that it cannot be used again
brace: a couple, or pair, usually of male/female animals
analogue watch: Clockwork watch. A self-winding watch relies on the
movements of the body to keep the spring fully wound
stashed: stored away (usually money or valuables) – a slang expression
keepsake: an object (given) to remember somebody by

Exploring the poem

(1) Imagine you are a police officer enquiring into the death of this man.
  - List the items found 'about his person'. What impression do they give you of
    a the man himself   **b** the possible reasons for his death?
  - Which aspects of the evidence seem clear to you? Why?
  - Which aspects of the evidence are you less sure about? Why?
  - What do you feel is the most important piece of evidence about the man?

  Support your answers with evidence from the poem.

Language

(2) Many of the items in the poem can be read as metaphors (see glossary, page 93) for death and violence, for example, the 'library card on its date of expiry'. Find and write out other lines which can be read in this way.

(3) Which lines made the strongest impression on you? Explain why.

(4) How many images of love and marriage can you find?

(5) Many of the words in the poem have more than one meaning.
  - What different meanings can you find in the title of the poem?
  - Read lines 9–14. How many different meanings can you find?
  - Explain the possible meanings of the final line of the poem.

Structure

(6) The poem is written in rhyming couplets (see glossary, page 93) and the opening couplets suggest a steady rhythm, or metre (see glossary, page 94). These features give a sense of order and regularity which reflects police methods.

Read the whole of the poem aloud to a steady beat and in a matter-of-fact voice. You should stress four vowel sounds (see glossary, page 95) in the longer lines and two vowel sounds in the shorter lines, for example:

  o /   o /   o o / o /
'A brace of keys for a mortise lock' (line 7)

  o / o o /
'A final demand' (line 9).

Aim for one beat per second, 63 seconds for the whole poem.
  - Is it possible to read the poem in a matter-of-fact voice and/or to a regular beat? Which lines cause difficulty and why?
  - What different things could the beat of the poem be compared with? Why?

(7) Comment on the way the poet has positioned the word 'ring'.

(8) Is the poem just a list of 'objects'? Which lines make it more than this, and why?

Writing

1   Is the poet writing about one person, more than one person, or all of us? Explain your view clearly.

2   Use your imagination to invent a series of 'documents', e.g. the 'shopping list', the 'final demand', the 'police report', which help to show what happened to the man.

The poems together

Interpretation

This **assessment objective** focuses on your ability to understand what the poems are about. Almost all poems in this section show an interest in the impressions which people and places can make on us. **It Ain't What You Do . . .**, for example, tries to capture the poetry and the feelings of moments that do not last, the **untitled poem** explores an experience where at least one person has been 'marked' for life, and **Poem** and **About His Person** look at impressions of people and our feelings about them after they have gone.

Poem and About His Person

1 Both poems give impressions of men who – for one reason or another – are no longer around, but we learn about each of them in a very different way. How do we find out about the man in each poem?

2 What do the poems suggest about each man's relationships with others?

3 What do the poems suggest about each man's values and lifestyle?

4 What do the poems suggest about the poet's attitude to each man?

5 How strong is your impression of each man and how do you respond to each of them?

Cataract Operation and It Ain't What You Do . . .

These poems reflect some of Simon Armitage's ideas about writing poetry.

6   Which aspects of each poem show you that the poet believes that poetry can be found in ordinary, everyday places and experiences?

7   Simon Armitage says (page 5): 'Poetry for me is a way of seeing the world. It's a way of making sense of the world and connecting with it.' Which features of each poem suggest that he is expressing this idea about the purposes of writing poetry?

8   What does **Cataract Operation** have to say about being 'clever' with images?

9   What does **It Ain't What You Do...** have to say about the images and experiences which we associate with adventure and travel?

Structure

Both **Poem** and the **untitled poem** share many of the features of a sonnet (see glossary, page 95). However, neither poem seems at first sight to fit the traditional idea of a sonnet, and each is very different from the other in its effect.

1   To what extent does the structure of each poem conform to the rules of the sonnet form?

2   To what extent does the subject matter of each poem reflect the sonnet tradition? For example, what does each poem show us about relationships and feelings?

3   Both poems feature rhyme, but in very different ways. How does the poet use rhyme in each of the poems? Comment on the different effects he achieves.

4   Which poem do you feel is the better example of the sonnet form and the traditions with which it is associated? Give your reasons.

Language

1   This poet's writing suggests a fascination with puns (see glossary, page 94) and with words and expressions which can be interpreted in more than one way. Using a dictionary if necessary, write down all the possible meanings of the following words. How many of these different meanings make sense in the context of the poem, and how do they contribute to your understanding?
   * butterfingered (**untitled poem**)
   * blind (**Cataract Operation**)
   * planted (**About His Person**)

Cataract Operation, It Ain't What You Do... and the untitled poem

2   Many of the images in these poems can be read as metaphors (see glossary, page 93). What do the following images suggest to you and how is each used?
   * the hens in **Cataract Operation**
   * the ripples and the light aircraft in **It Ain't What You Do...**
   * the burning rings in the **untitled poem**.

Sample questions

When examiners write questions, they are giving you opportunities to meet specific **assessment objectives**. Before you answer any of the questions on this page, look at question 1 below and the model answer plan opposite.

In the examination you have only 30 minutes to answer a question on the poems of Simon Armitage. The model answer plan is structured in a way which helps you understand and address clearly the key assessment objectives on which the question is focused:

- interpretation
- language
- structure.

---

1 What kinds of feelings are expressed in **It Ain't What You Do**... and the **untitled poem**? You should write about:

develop and sustain an interpretation

- the *range* of feelings in *each poem* — *make cross-references*

understand and evaluate linguistic devices

- the ways the poet uses *language* and *structure* to express these. — *understand and evaluate structural devices*

---

2 Both **About His Person** and **Poem** present the reader with impressions of people after they have gone. What impressions are given and how are these created?

3 Write about **two** poems from this section which have interested you because of the way the poet uses language. You should consider:
- interesting uses of language in each poem
- how these add to your understanding of the poems.

4 Choose at least **two** poems in which the poet seems to be exploring his ideas about writing poetry. Write about:
- the ideas
- how each poem puts across these ideas.

5 In what ways do **Cataract Operation** and **About His Person** show that appearances can be deceptive?

Model answer plan

What kinds of feelings are expressed in **It Ain't What You Do...** and the **untitled poem**? You should write about:

- the range of feelings in each poem
- the ways the poet uses language and structure to express these.

Plan	Examiner's observations
Begin by establishing the idea that both poems are trying to capture feelings which are not straightforward or easy to express and that both poems explore a range of feelings, each in a different way.	This establishes a clear focus on the question. By identifying something which both poems have in common you have also made a cross-reference and set an agenda for your response.
Untitled Poem The poem begins and ends in the present, but the middle sections recall the past. Make the point that it is this aspect of the poem's structure which enables the poet to explore the range of the person's feelings.	Identifying the structure of the poem helps to show how it develops. You don't have to work through the poem line by line to show this! Remember that the main focus of the question is on 'feelings'.
Explain in detail what the poet's use of language, in the middle sections, suggests about how the person felt at the time. For example: • the rhyming of 'name' with 'flame' • the poet's choice of words • the middle stanza as a metaphor for marriage. A close look at the final stanza will help you to explore what the person feels now. You could discuss: • what the expression 'butterfingered' suggests about the person's feelings, past and present • how the poet emphasises the words 'marked' and 'at thirteen' and what this shows you about the person's feelings now.	Once you have identified how the structure works, you can go on to look more closely at the poet's use of language. It's not enough to identify a metaphor or the fact that something rhymes. You should try to evaluate how the language shows us the range of feelings. Finishing your discussion with a focus on the last few lines of the poem will help show your understanding of how it develops.
It Ain't What You Do... Begin by commenting on how this poem also uses sound patterns and images to capture feelings. Go on to make the point that in this poem the range of feelings is expressed by looking at how the person and others feel in different places. You could now write about: • his enjoyment of the stillness and peace of Black Moss, and how this tranquillity is captured by the sound patterns he uses • the 'Taj Mahal' stanza as a metaphor for the feelings he is describing when he skims the stone • his feelings when holding the boy's head in the day centre and how the images in this stanza help to show you what he is feeling.	It's important to select the relevant material – you haven't got time to discuss the whole poem. Note how the discussion picks up from where it left off by focusing immediately on language. By commenting on a similarity and a difference another cross-reference is made. It's important that when you give more than one example of something, you don't simply repeat the same points; try to use any further examples to develop your points or to show different feelings.
By exploring how stanzas in the poem can be seen as metaphors for feelings, you have shown a clear understanding of how the poem develops.	By exploring successive feelings in the poem, you have traced the development of the poet's ideas and sustained an interpretation.

② Carol Ann Duffy

Carol Ann Duffy was born in Glasgow in 1955. She grew up in Staffordshire and went to university in Liverpool. Having spent some time in London as a freelance writer, she now lives in Manchester.

She has won many prizes and received several awards for her poetry. Her collections of poems include:

- *Standing Female Nude* (Anvil Press, 1985)
- *The Other Country* (Anvil Press, 1990), for which she received a Scottish Arts Council Book Award
- *Selling Manhattan* (Anvil Press, 1987), which earned her a Somerset Maugham Award in 1988
- *Mean Time* (Anvil Press, 1993), which received both the Forward Poetry Prize and the Whitbread Poetry Award for 1993.

Carol Ann Duffy started writing poetry when she was at school. She was encouraged by an English teacher who typed up her teenage poems and helped her to get some of them published. She cannot single out one particular poet as a special favourite – she likes too many!

The poet Ted Hughes believes that all writers search for a 'perfect place' to write in; Carol Ann Duffy writes her poems in her study at home. She writes them by hand in a notebook, typing them out later. She sees the writing of poetry as a 'vocation', a special calling, and any other kind of writing is done to subsidize her poetry writing.

Her poems, she says, 'come from my everyday experience, my past/memory and my imagination. People and characters are fascinating to me'. This will become clear to you as you read the following five poems, all of which focus on people and relationships.

These poems are all based on true experiences and real people. Mrs Tilscher was Carol Ann Duffy's teacher in her last year at junior school when she took her Eleven Plus (an examination which children sat in their final year at junior school to decide whether they moved on to a grammar school or not). Everything that she describes in **In Mrs Tilscher's Class** (from *The Other Country*, 1990) is true.

Strange as it may seem, the events in **Stealing** (from *Selling Manhattan*, 1987) are also true. Carol Ann Duffy lived in an area in which there were a lot of burglaries, and a snowman really was stolen! She invented a character for the thief.

She wrote **Valentine** (from *Mean Time*, 1993) so that she could give it, along with the onion, to her lover on Valentine's Day.

In the 1970s Carol Ann Duffy was friendly with Don McCullin, a famous photographer whose photographs of war were widely published and respected. Her poem, **War Photographer**, (from *Standing Female Nude*, 1985), is based on conversations she had with him.

Before You Were Mine (from *Mean Time*, 1993) is a poem about her mother's teenage years in Scotland, going to dances, having boyfriends and so on. She refers in the poem to this famous photograph of Marilyn Monroe, an association triggered by a similar photograph of her mother, also called Marilyn, as a carefree teenager.

War Photographer

In his darkroom he is finally alone
with spools of suffering set out in ordered rows.
The only light is red and softly glows,
as though this were a church and he
5   a priest preparing to intone a Mass.
Belfast. Beirut. Phnom Penh. All flesh is grass.

He has a job to do. Solutions slop in trays
beneath his hands which did not tremble then
though seem to now. Rural England. Home again
10 to ordinary pain which simple weather can dispel,
to fields which don't explode beneath the feet
of running children in a nightmare heat.

Something is happening. A stranger's features
faintly start to twist before his eyes,
15 a half-formed ghost. He remembers the cries
of this man's wife, how he sought approval
without words to do what someone must
and how the blood stained into foreign dust.

A hundred agonies in black-and-white
20 from which his editor will pick out five or six
for Sunday's supplement. The reader's eyeballs prick
with tears between the bath and pre-lunch beers.
From the aeroplane he stares impassively at where
he earns his living and they do not care.

Exploring the poem

1. List in sequence the different things that happen in the poem.

2. What do the following extracts from the poem say about the way the photographer feels about his job?

   a 'He has a job to do.' (line 7)

   b 'beneath his hands which did not tremble then
      though seem to now.' (lines 8–9)

   c '...how he sought approval
      without words to do what someone must' (lines 16–17)

   d '...he stares impassively at where
      he earns his living and they do not care.' (lines 23–24)

3. Which of the following statements do you agree with? Find evidence from the poem to support your views.

   a The poet is criticizing the photographer for what he does.

   b The poet admires the photographer for what he does.

   c The photographer is sickened by what he does but feels it is his duty.

Structure

4. The poem is written in four stanzas (see glossary, page 95) of six lines each, with the same rhyme scheme (see glossary, page 95). Sum up in a sentence what each stanza tells you about the photographer.

5. There are two contrasting worlds in this poem: the world of war zones and the calmer world of 'Rural England'. The war photographer is the man who goes between these two worlds.

   Where do you think the photographer would rather be: out in the war zones doing his job, or back in the safety of England? Use evidence from the poem to support your view.

Language

6. Words and phrases can be connected by rhyme (see glossary, page 95). Look at the following examples. Why do you think the poet rhymed them?

   • 'intone a Mass' (line 5) / 'All flesh is grass' (line 6)

   • 'did not tremble then' (line 8) / 'Home again' (line 9)

Writing

1. What view of war photographers is presented in this poem? How is this achieved? Think about:

   • the language the poet uses

   • the way she sets out her ideas.

2. Imagine that the war photographer keeps a journal in which he records what he sees, what he does and how he feels about it.

   Write two entries that might appear in his journal. One should be written when he is at work and one when he is at home.

Valentine

Not a red rose or a satin heart.

I give you an onion.
It is a moon wrapped in brown paper.
It promises light
5   like the careful undressing of love.

Here.
It will blind you with tears
like a lover.
It will make your reflection
10   a wobbling photo of grief.

I am trying to be truthful.

Not a cute card or a kissogram.

I give you an onion.
Its fierce kiss will stay on your lips,
15   possessive and faithful
as we are,
for as long as we are.

Take it.
Its platinum loops shrink to a wedding-ring,
20   if you like.
Lethal.
Its scent will cling to your fingers,
cling to your knife.

Explanations

satin: a glossy fabric
platinum: a precious metal
considered more valuable than gold
Lethal: causing death

Exploring the poem

1. What would you expect to read in a poem called **Valentine**? How is this poem similar or different to what you would expect?

Language

2. The poet uses an extended metaphor (see glossary, page 93) which describes something (her relationship) as if it is the thing it resembles (an onion). Use the table below to explore the metaphor.

Stages of the metaphor	Reference	What the poet is saying
An onion is light underneath a darker outer skin.	lines 2–5	As a relationship unfolds, different aspects of a person are revealed.
Onions make a person's eyes water.		
Raw onions leave a strong taste on the lips.		
Onions are made up of rings.		
The smell of an onion lingers on the skin.		
Onions are chopped up.		

3. What do these words tell you about the poet's feelings about the relationship?
   - promises (line 4)
   - blind (line 7)
   - fierce (line 14)
   - shrink (line 19)
   - cling (line 23)

4. In what ways is **Valentine** an effective title for the poem? What would the poem lose or gain if it was titled **Onion**?

Structure

5. The poem is structured into stanzas and lines of different length.
   - Is there a connection between the three single lines (lines 1, 11, 12)?
   - Why do you think the poet chose to put 'Here.', 'Take it.' and 'Lethal.' on lines of their own?
   - What impact does the final line have?

Writing

1. What view of love is developed in the poem?
   Consider:
   - the different aspects of love revealed in the poem
   - how the metaphor of the onion helps the poet develop her ideas.

2. The poet uses the extended metaphor of the onion to explore her feelings about a relationship.
   Write a poem using a metaphor, such as a ship on a journey or a flower bud opening.

3. Write a story called **Valentine** which, like the poem, doesn't go in the direction a reader might expect.

Stealing

The most unusual thing I ever stole? A snowman.
Midnight. He looked magnificent; a tall, white mute
beneath the winter moon. I wanted him, a mate
with a mind as cold as the slice of ice
5   within my own brain. I started with the head.

Better off dead than giving in, not taking
what you want. He weighed a ton; his torso,
frozen stiff, hugged to my chest, a fierce chill
piercing my gut. Part of the thrill was knowing
10 that children would cry in the morning. Life's tough.

Sometimes I steal things I don't need. I joy-ride cars
to nowhere, break into houses just to have a look.
I'm a mucky ghost, leave a mess, maybe pinch a camera.
I watch my gloved hand twisting the doorknob.
15 A stranger's bedroom. Mirrors. I sigh like this – *Aah*.

It took some time. Reassembled in the yard,
he didn't look the same. I took a run
and booted him. Again. Again. My breath ripped out
in rags. It seems daft now. Then I was standing
20 alone amongst lumps of snow, sick of the world.

Boredom. Mostly I'm so bored I could eat myself.
One time, I stole a guitar and thought I might
learn to play. I nicked a bust of Shakespeare once,
flogged it, but the snowman was strangest.
25 You don't understand a word I'm saying, do you?

Explanations

mute: a person unable to talk
torso: the upper half of the body
a bust of Shakespeare: a statue of Shakespeare's head and shoulders
flogged: 1 whipped or beaten **2** sold

Exploring the poem

1. The first and last lines of the poem show that the thief is talking to someone. Imagine you are a social worker who has to prepare a report about the thief. Make notes for your report under the following headings:

    a Items stolen

    b His/her anti-social feelings

    c My impressions (of the thief).

Structure

2. The poet writes this poem from a particular point of view. The 'voice' of the poem is that of the thief. Each stanza (see glossary, page 95) develops our understanding of the thief.

    - Read the first two stanzas. Why does the thief steal the snowman?
    - The third stanza gives some further information about the thief. Why does s/he steal?
    - The fourth stanza tells what s/he did with the stolen snowman. What happened, and why?
    - The last stanza gives another reason for the theft of the snowman. What is this?
    - What does the last line of the poem reveal about the thief?

Language

3. The poem begins and ends with the thief talking directly to someone. What words/phrases can you find in the poem to show that it is conversational?

4. The snowman is an object stolen by the thief. How is it described? Is the language used to describe it conversational?

5. The sounds of words are important to the poet. The phrase 'the slice of ice' may be said with a hiss which emphasizes the cold absence of ordinary human emotions. Alliteration (see glossary, page 93) can emphasize key words:

    - Comment on the use of words beginning with 'm' in the first stanza.
    - What is the effect of the similarity between 'mute' and 'mate'?

6. How would you read aloud 'I sigh like this – *Aah*.'

    - mockingly   •   sadly   •   sarcastically   •   sincerely   •   angrily?

    Support your answer with evidence from the poem.

Writing

1. In **Stealing** the poet presents a picture of an outsider, someone who doesn't fit into society. Write about:

    - what you learn about the thief
    - the connection between the snowman and the thief
    - how the poet presents this picture convincingly.

2. Imagine you are someone who doesn't really fit in, for example, a homeless person living on the streets, or someone in trouble with the police.

    - What sort of things would you do?
    - What would you think about other people who do seem to 'fit in'?

Before You Were Mine

I'm ten years away from the corner you laugh on
with your pals, Maggie McGeeney and Jean Duff.
The three of you bend from the waist, holding
each other, or your knees, and shriek at the pavement.
5 Your polka-dot dress blows round your legs. Marilyn.

I'm not here yet. The thought of me doesn't occur
in the ballroom with the thousand eyes, the fizzy, movie
    tomorrows
the right walk home could bring. I knew you would dance
10 like that. Before you were mine, your Ma stands at the close
with a hiding for the late one. You reckon it's worth it.

The decade ahead of my loud, possessive yell was the best
    one, eh?
I remember my hands in those high-heeled red shoes, relics,
15 and now your ghost clatters toward me over George Square
till I see you, clear as scent, under the tree,
with its lights, and whose small bites on your neck,
    sweetheart?

Cha cha cha! You'd teach me the steps on the way home from
20 Mass,
stamping stars from the wrong pavement. Even then
I wanted the bold girl winking in Portobello, somewhere
in Scotland, before I was born. That glamorous love lasts
where you sparkle and waltz and laugh before you were
25 mine.

Explanations

Maggie McGeeney, Jean Duff: two friends of the poet's mother

polka-dot: a pattern of regularly spaced circular dots

Marilyn: the poet's mother. This famous photograph of Marilyn Monroe shows her skirt billowing up in a hot air current

relics: a relic is something that has survived from the past. It often means something that is treasured

George Square: a place in Glasgow

Cha cha cha!: a dance

Portobello: a small town near Edinburgh

Exploring the poem

1. Read the first three stanzas (see glossary, page 95) carefully and put together a picture of what the poet's mother, Marilyn, was like. Refer to details of the poem for each question:
   - What kind of clothes did she wear?
   - What kinds of things did she enjoy doing?
   - What was her attitude to life?

2. In line 14 and in the last stanza the poet remembers scenes from her childhood.
   - What did the poet like and admire about her mother?
   - Do you think motherhood changed Marilyn? Give reasons for your views.

3. Why do you think the poet has 'Marilyn' (line 5) as a one-word sentence?

4. What do you think is meant by

   '... the fizzy, movie
       tomorrows
   the right walk home could bring.' (lines 7–9)?

5. The poet describes her memory of being a child in Glasgow and her mother teaching her to cha cha as 'stamping stars from the wrong pavement' (line 21). What do you think this means?

Structure

6. There are several references to time in this poem. Marilyn appears at three different times:

   a ten years before the birth of her daughter

   b when her daughter was a little girl

   c in the poet's mind now.

   Find the references to these times in the poem. How would you sum up the poet's view of her mother at each of those times?

Language

7. Find the following phrases in the poem. Comment on the poet's choice of the underlined words. What impression is she trying to create?
   - 'and <u>shriek</u> at the pavement'
   - 'the <u>fizzy</u>, movie tomorrows'
   - 'my loud, <u>possessive</u> yell'
   - 'your ghost <u>clatters</u> towards me'
   - 'clear <u>as scent</u>'
   - '<u>stamping</u> stars'.

Writing

1. How does the poet communicate her feelings for her mother? Consider:
   - what those feelings are and how they are developed through the poem
   - how the poet uses language to bring the description of her mother to life.

2. Write about someone you are close to. Is there a particularly important part of their life that took place before you knew them?

In Mrs Tilscher's Class

You could travel up the Blue Nile
with your finger, tracing the route
while Mrs Tilscher chanted the scenery.
Tana. Ethiopia. Khartoum. Aswân.
5   That for an hour, then a skittle of milk
and the chalky Pyramids rubbed into dust.
A window opened with a long pole.
The laugh of a bell swung by a running child.

This was better than home. Enthralling books.
10 The classroom glowed like a sweet shop.
Sugar paper. Coloured shapes. Brady and Hindley
faded, like the faint, uneasy smudge of a mistake.
Mrs Tilscher loved you. Some mornings, you found
she'd left a good gold star by your name.
15 The scent of a pencil slowly, carefully, shaved.
A xylophone's nonsense heard from another form.

Over the Easter term, the inky tadpoles changed
from commas into exclamation marks. Three frogs
hopped in the playground, freed by a dunce,
20 followed by a line of kids, jumping and croaking
away from the lunch queue. A rough boy
told you how you were born. You kicked him, but stared
at your parents, appalled, when you got back home.

That feverish July, the air tasted of electricity.
25 A tangible alarm made you always untidy, hot,
fractious under the heavy, sexy sky. You asked her
how you were born and Mrs Tilscher smiled,
then turned away. Reports were handed out.
You ran through the gates, impatient to be grown,
30 as the sky split open into a thunderstorm.

Explanations

Tana. Ethiopia. Khartoum. Aswân: places in Africa around the Nile. Tana is a lake in Ethiopia. Khartoum is a city in the Sudan and Aswân is in Egypt

skittle of milk: schoolchildren used to be given a small, chubby bottle of free milk every day

Brady and Hindley: Ian Brady and Myra Hindley, known as the Moors Murderers, were found guilty of the abduction and murder of children in 1966

tangible: capable of being touched or felt, definite

fractious: irritable

Exploring the poem

1. The first two stanzas (see glossary, page 95) paint a picture of a primary school classroom in the 1960s. Make a list of the different things the poet can remember.

2. How did the poet feel about:
   - her primary school days • her teacher?

3. The last two stanzas describe how things changed.
   - How did the tadpoles change?
   - How did what the 'rough boy' said change things?
   - How did the weather change?

4. How are these changes, and the fact that Mrs Tilscher 'turned away', linked to growing up?

Structure

5. At first glance the stanzas seem to be of equal length, but there are differences: the first two are eight lines long and the final two are seven lines long.

   Why do you think the poet changed the structure like this after line 16?

Language

6. Images are word pictures painted by poets. Try to explain the following images and say why you think the poet has chosen them.
   - 'a skittle of milk' (line 5) • 'The laugh of a bell' (line 8)
   - 'The classroom glowed like a sweetshop' (line 10)

7. How does the following simile help you understand the poet's reaction to Brady and Hindley?

   'Brady and Hindley / faded, like the faint, uneasy smudge of a mistake' (lines 11–12)

   Why do you think the poet chose to compare tadpoles with these punctuation marks?

   '...the inky tadpoles changed / from commas into exclamation marks' (lines 17–18)

8. What do you think the 'thunderstorm' (line 30) represents?

9. Poets choose their words very carefully – poetry was once described as 'the best words in the best order'. Comment on the underlined words:
   - 'You could travel up the Blue Nile' (line 1)
   - 'The classroom glowed' (line 10)
   - 'she'd left a good gold star by your name' (line 14)
   - 'A xylophone's nonsense' (line 16)
   - 'That feverish July' (line 24) • 'the heavy, sexy sky' (line 26)

Writing

1. This poem tells a story in which things change greatly between the beginning and the end. Write about these changes and the way the poet describes them.

2. Write about your memories of primary school. Describe what it was like and try to capture how you felt at the time. Think about:
   - sights • smells • what you did • your feelings.

The poems together

Interpretation

This **assessment objective** focuses on your ability to understand what the poems are about. You should identify the subject matter and the poet's approach to it. A feature of the five poems you have looked at is an interest in people and relationships. You could examine:

- which people seem to be the focus of each poem
- which poems seem to be more about relationships than individuals
- whether there are any poems in which the poet seems more interested in something other than people and relationships.

War Photographer and Stealing

The characters in both of these poems are outsiders.

1 What do the photographer and the thief do which makes them outsiders?
2 From whose point of view is each poem developed?
3 What seems to be the poet's attitude towards the characters? How does she present them to the reader?

Valentine and Before You Were Mine

Both of these poems are about relationships but of very different kinds.

4 What are the relationships being described in each of the poems?
5 Are there any significant similarities and differences in the poet's attitude to and treatment of the relationship in each case?

Structure

To get high marks you must not only identify features of structure but also show how it shapes the ideas of the poem.

1 What similarities can you see in the stanza patterns of **War Photographer, Stealing, Before You Were Mine** and **In Mrs Tilscher's Class**?

Stealing and Valentine

2 In terms of shape, what does each stanza of **Stealing** have in common?

3 In each stanza quite long sentences run on from line to line. Why might the poet have split the following lines like this?

   a '...I joy-ride cars
     to nowhere' (lines 11–12)

   b '...Then I was standing
     alone amongst lumps of snow' (lines 19–20).

4 Why has the poet split lines 3, 4 and 5 as she has?

5 Choose three short sentences and comment on their effectiveness.

6 Explain why the poet splits lines 4–5 and 15–17 of **Valentine** as she does.

7 The poem seems formless, with a mixture of long and short lines. Try to explain
   - why line 19 is the longest line of the poem
   - why 'Here.' and 'Take it.' are on lines of their own.

8 Can you see any similarities in the poet's approach to structure in **Valentine** and **Stealing**? What are they?

Language

In Mrs Tilscher's Class and Before You Were Mine

1 Think about the poet's choice of 'inky', 'commas' and 'exclamation marks' to describe the tadpoles in **In Mrs Tilscher's Class**. How effective is the punctuation metaphor (see glossary, page 93)?

2 What is the effect of the alliteration (see glossary, page 93) in 'Three frogs... freed... followed' (lines 18–20)?

3 Who or what is 'jumping and croaking' (line 20)?

4 Much of the description in **In Mrs Tilscher's Class** is in metaphors. Compare that approach with the ways the poet describes people in **Before You Were Mine**:
   - What is the effect of verbs like 'shriek', 'clatter', 'stamping', 'sparkle' and 'waltz'?
   - Why is much of the language colloquial?

Valentine, Stealing and In Mrs Tilscher's Class

5 The poet uses metaphors in these poems in different ways and for different effects. How does she use the onion in **Valentine**, the snowman in **Stealing** and the weather in **In Mrs Tilscher's Class**?

Stealing and War Photographer

6 How does the poet use the sounds of words to convey atmosphere and shape her meaning in the opening stanzas of **Stealing** and **War Photographer**? Think about:
   - assonance (see glossary, page 93)
   - rhyme (see glossary, page 95)
   - alliteration (see glossary, page 93)

Sample questions

When examiners write questions, they are giving you opportunities to meet specific **assessment objectives**. Before you answer any of the questions on this page, look at question 1 below and the model answer plan opposite.

In the examination you have only 30 minutes to answer a question on the poems of Carol Ann Duffy. The model answer plan is structured in a way which helps you understand and address clearly the key assessment objectives on which the question is focused:

- interpretation
- language
- structure.

---

make cross-references

develop and sustain an interpretation

understand and evaluate linguistic devices

understand and evaluate structural devices

1 **Valentine** and **In Mrs Tilscher's Class** show how things can change. Show how the poet explores change in *each* of the poems. Comment on:

- *the kinds of change she explores*
- the *language* she uses
- how the *structure* of the poems affects your response to them.

---

2 Write about the ways Carol Ann Duffy explores relationships in her poems. Consider:
- the different kinds of relationships
- the effect of the different ways the poems are set out
- the interesting ways she uses language.

3 Explain how Carol Ann Duffy conveys her feelings towards the 'outsiders' in **War Photographer** and **Stealing**. Write about:
- her attitude towards the photographer and the thief
- how these feelings are reflected in the language and structure of each poem
- your own response.

4 Write about **two** of the poems which especially interested you. Comment on:
- the ideas presented in the poems
- interesting features of language
- your own response to the poems.

5 Many of Carol Ann Duffy's poems are about people. Choose **two** poems in which particular people are described and explain how the structure and language of each poem make the people interesting.

Model answer plan

1 **Valentine** and **In Mrs Tilscher's Class** show how things can change. Show how the poet explores change in each of the poems. Comment on:
   - the kinds of change she explores
   - the language she uses
   - how the structure of the poems affects your response to them.

Plan	Examiner's observations
Valentine Begin with some discussion of how the relationship changed. Establish that it is a poem looking at how love changes.	This focuses clearly on the key aspect of the question, i.e. change.
Continue with discussion of some particularly interesting uses of language. For example, the effectiveness of words and phrases such as 'cute card', 'fierce kiss' and 'shrink'; the details of the extended metaphor such as 'the careful undressing of love' (line 5) which focus on how the relationship has changed. Show how the use of language enhances meaning. The poet uses the metaphor of an onion to reflect the changing aspects of the relationship, which moves from promise through different stages such as grief to something quite harmful at the end.	Discuss these different stages and include some comment on: • the way the poem is written in separate sections, moving between metaphor and straight talking • the way the poet uses long and short lines. This section is looking at structure. You may worry that imagery is more to do with language than structure, but in this case the poet uses the onion metaphor to structure her ideas and to shape the way you respond to her views.
In Mrs Tilscher's Class Although this could be viewed as a poem which explores a change in relationships it is more a poem about a life change: a child's view of the world changing. You mustn't feel that you have to find similarities; these two poems are about different kinds of change.	Try to develop a consistent view of the poem. The first two stanzas describe a state of contentment and innocence: explore some of the details. There is then a change: the last two stanzas describe the event which brought about the change and its consequences. You could point out how the last two stanzas are actually a different length from the first two.
Look at the structure – the shape of the poem.	You'll gain few marks for noting it is in four stanzas; more marks for linking shape to ideas.
Discuss the images of the poem: • some focus on change (the tadpoles, the weather) • some establish pleasure – in the first two stanzas • others suggest tension.	Look at the way the choice of vocabulary changes the mood of the poem. Try to link your observations about language back to the main focus of the question – change.

③ Ted Hughes

Ted Hughes is one of Britain's best-known poets. He became Poet Laureate on 19 December 1984. He has written several books of poetry for adults and children. Many young people also know of him through reading some of the many stories he has written, such as **The Iron Man**.

Ted Hughes was born in 1930 in Mytholmroyd, a small town in West Yorkshire, not far from Halifax. He has memories of growing up in the days before television: his only book, until he reached the age of eight, was an encyclopedia of animals. When he was eight his family moved to Mexborough, a mining town in South Yorkshire, where his parents took over a newsagent's and tobacconist's shop. That gave him access to the boys' magazines and comics which he read as they appeared in the shop.

His love of poetry developed at grammar school: 'It dawned on me that rhymes were far more interesting than prose.' One of the main things that appealed to him about poetry was rhythm, and he remembers how he was particularly attracted to verse written in strong rhythms. He enjoyed the poetry of Rudyard Kipling and sections of the King James Bible, but he has a special memory of the Irish poet W. B. Yeats, and one of his poems in particular, **The Wanderings of Oisin**. As you read the five poems in the **NEAB English Anthology** you will see for yourself how important rhythm still is to Ted Hughes.

By the age of seventeen he knew he wanted to be a poet and to earn a living through writing. He went to university to study English but changed to Anthropology (the study of humans – their origins and the way they organize themselves) because he felt it would help him more in his writing. After university he had a succession of jobs, including working in a zoo, as a nightwatchman and in the script-reading department at Pinewood Film Studios. Then he won a prestigious poetry prize which enabled him to travel to America where he worked as a teacher, with his first wife, the poet Sylvia Plath. Since then he has earned his living as a writer.

Ted Hughes has this to say about why he writes poems:

'When I am asked why I write poems I have to say – because I find myself wanting to write them. I have wanted to write them since I was about fifteen, and I go on wanting to write them. But what that "something" is, that needs to be expressed, is not easy to know – until you have expressed it. I rarely have more than a very rough plan for what I hope to write next. And in practice, what comes up is usually a surprise, often totally different from what I thought I was looking for.'

He recognizes that many people see no point in poetry and he believes that the main reason for this is because of the way poetry is often read:

'They read it as if it were instructions on how to operate a washing machine. Or as if it were a postcard from a friend on holiday. Or as if they were just talking casually to keep a conversation going. All such ways of speaking fall within the range of a person's "normal" voice. But the same person has a different kind of voice, waiting for its moment. When they get into a quarrel with somebody they love dearly – then you hear that other voice. As if their whole body were trying to speak. Or when they are calling (God forbid they ever need to!) from the window of a burning house. Or when they are on the telephone trying to persuade a certain person to join them in some fabulous place. This other way of speaking belongs just as truly to that same person. Or perhaps, even more truly. Because when a person is speaking out of a crisis, as in these instances, they put far more of themselves into their voice and into what they say. You could say they speak with greater feeling, but it is more than that.'

Finding that voice, he feels, is the key to learning to read and write poetry.

Ted Hughes can remember exactly where he was when he wrote most of his poems. **Wind** is the only one of the five in this section which was written in more than one place and over a long period of time. It began as a description of a football match in Heptonstall in West Yorkshire but lay untouched for a couple of years before he returned to it, got rid of the football match and focused instead on the weather. He remembers living in a house up in the Pennines 'where the horizontal rain would be driven against the walls so hard – strong built, stone walls, not very old – that the rain would come bubbling through the wallpaper on the inside'.

Hawk Roosting was written while he was living in Boston in America. He remembers writing the poem 'as fast as I could write' and he didn't alter a word of it afterwards. He wrote it after seeing a hawk flying over Boston, which reminded him of a failed earlier attempt to write about a young sparrowhawk he had caught and tried to keep alive when he was a boy.

The machine in **Tractor** was Ted Hughes's old blue Fordson. The poem arose out of his 'fight' with the temperamental tractor one cold morning when he wanted to clean out the cattle shed. He wrote the poem in his writer's den – a hut in an orchard in Devon.

Work and Play, like **The Warm and the Cold** was part of a collection of poems for a children's festival, a group of poems called *Season Songs* with pieces for each season. It was written during a heatwave in 1974. Ted Hughes says it 'revolves around a contrast, playful I hope, between two ways of coping with the demands of infants and a very hot summer'.

The Warm and the Cold was written over two to three days while standing at a lectern in the upstairs bedroom of his house in Devon and while walking by the local river. Ted Hughes imagined the poem 'as a kind of tapestry of a medieval landscape, in which creatures living in the naked elements, through a deep freeze that some of them might in actuality not survive, appear as cosy, happy, comforting things'.

Work and Play

The swallow of summer, she toils all the summer,
A blue-dark knot of glittering voltage,
A whiplash swimmer, a fish of the air.
      But the serpent of cars that crawls through the dust
5   In shimmering exhaust
      Searching to slake
      Its fever in ocean
      Will play and be idle or else it will bust.

The swallow of summer, the barbed harpoon,
10 She flings from the furnace, a rainbow of purples,
Dips her glow in the pond and is perfect.
      But the serpent of cars that collapsed on the beach
      Disgorges its organs
      A scamper of colours
15   Which roll like tomatoes
      Nude as tomatoes
      With sand in their creases
      To cringe in the sparkle of rollers and screech.

The swallow of summer, the seamstress of summer,
20 She scissors the blue into shapes and she sews it,
She draws a long thread and she knots it at corners.
      But the holiday people
      Are laid out like wounded
      Flat as in ovens
25   Roasting and basting
      With faces of torment as space burns them blue
      Their heads are transistors
      Their teeth grit on sand grains
      Their lost kids are squalling
30   While man-eating flies
      Jab electric shock needles but what can they do?

They can climb in their cars with raw bodies, raw faces
      And start up the serpent
      And headache it homeward
35   A car full of squabbles
      And sobbing and stickiness
      With sand in their crannies
      Inhaling petroleum
      That pours from the foxgloves
40   While the evening swallow
The swallow of summer, cartwheeling through crimson,
Touches the honey-slow river and turning
Returns to the hand stretched from under the eaves –
A boomerang of rejoicing shadow.

Explanations

serpent: a snake

slake: pour water on

barbed harpoon: a large throwing-spear with barbed point and a rope attached, used for hunting whales

disgorges: throws out, vomits

rollers: large waves breaking on the beach

seamstress: a woman who sews and makes clothes

crannies: narrow openings, secret places

eaves: the part of a roof that projects beyond the walls

Exploring the poem

1. List all the different qualities of the swallow mentioned in the poem. Put them in a chart like the one below, with a line reference for each one.

Qualities	Line reference
the swallow works	line 1
the swallow is compact and energetic	line 2

2. Make a similar table for the holiday-makers.

Qualities	Line reference
the holiday-makers play	line 8

3. Which does the poet appear to admire more – the swallow or the holiday-makers? Give clear reasons for your answer.

Structure

4. In the first three stanzas (see glossary, page 95) the opening three lines describe the swallow. Why do you think the number of lines about the holiday-makers increases in each stanza?

5. How is the structure of the final stanza different? Why do you think the poet changes the structure here?

6. If you read the poem aloud you will realize that it has a strong rhythm (see glossary, page 95). The rhythm comes from a pattern of stressed and unstressed syllables (see glossary, page 95). This pattern is called the metre (see glossary, page 94).

   The rhythm can be marked by using / for a stressed syllable and ° for one that is not stressed.

   For example, the first line may be marked as follows:

   > °   / ° ° / ° ° / ° ° / °
   > 'The swallow of summer, she toils all the summer,'

   This shows that there are four stresses in the line and that there is a pattern of ° ° / which is repeated.

   Mark the unstressed and stressed syllables in some lines which describe the swallow and some which describe the holiday-makers.

   - What are the differences and similarities between the two?
   - In the third stanza (lines 19–31), how does the poet use rhythm and sound to emphasize the differences between the swallow and the holiday-makers?

Language

(7) In line 2, the swallow is described as 'a blue-dark knot'.

This image suggests a small compact creature, a little, tight bundle, unlike the long string of cars; 'blue-dark' instead of the usual 'dark blue' emphasizes the special nature of the bird.

What do the following images suggest about the swallow?
- 'the barbed harpoon' (line 9)
- 'the seamstress of summer' (line 19)
- 'A boomerang of rejoicing shadow' (line 44)

(8) The traffic queue is compared to a 'serpent' (lines 4, 12, 33). Comment on the effectiveness of this image.

(9) There are several references in the poem to fire and heat.

the swallow	the holiday-makers
'glittering voltage'	'fever'
'She flings from the furnace'	'Roasting and basting'
'Dips her glow in the pond'	'space burns them blue'

Comment on the differences between these and how they influence your view of
- the swallow
- the holiday-makers.

(10) Explain what is unusual about each of the following phrases.
- 'a rainbow of purples' (line 10)
- 'A scamper of colours' (line 14)
- 'headache it homeward' (line 34)
- 'petroleum / That pours from the foxgloves' (lines 38–9).

Why do you think the poet has chosen to use the words in this way?

Oral work

Prepare a small group reading of the poem. Decide how many different voices you need and in what tones you will read it to draw out the different views of the swallow and the holiday-makers.

Writing

1 Write about the contrasts in the poem. You should consider:
- the contrasts between the swallow and the holiday-makers
- the ways the poet uses language and structure to emphasize them.

2 Describe a place using contrast, which is an important feature of good descriptive writing. For example, you could describe the warm interior of a house and contrast it with the cold outside; or the bustle of a motorway with the snug calm of an animal's burrow.

The Warm and the Cold

Freezing dusk is closing
    Like a slow trap of steel
On trees and roads and hills and all
    That can no longer feel.
5   But the carp is in its depth
          Like a planet in its heaven.
          And the badger in its bedding
          Like a loaf in the oven.
          And the butterfly in its mummy
10   Like a viol in its case.
          And the owl in its feathers
          Like a doll in its lace.

Freezing dusk has tightened
    Like a nut screwed tight
15 On the starry aeroplane
    Of the soaring night.
          But the trout is in its hole
          Like a chuckle in a sleeper.
          The hare strays down the highway
20   Like a root going deeper.
          The snail is dry in the outhouse
          Like a seed in a sunflower.
          The owl is pale on the gatepost
          Like a clock on its tower.

25 Moonlight freezes the shaggy world
    Like a mammoth of ice –
The past and the future
    Are the jaws of a steel vice.
          But the cod is in the tide-rip
30   Like a key in a purse.
          The deer are on the bare-blown hill
          Like smiles on a nurse.
          The flies are behind the plaster
          Like the lost score of a jig.
35   Sparrows are in the ivy-clump
          Like money in a pig.

Such a frost
    The flimsy moon
          Has lost her wits.

40   A star falls.

The sweating farmers
    Turn in their sleep
          Like oxen on spits.

Explanations

dusk: the onset of night

carp: a freshwater fish

mummy: a preserved body, or the case in which it is kept; a pulpy substance

viol: a medieval stringed instrument, like a violin

chuckle: a quiet, private laugh

mammoth: a large, extinct, elephant-like creature with a shaggy coat. Their bodies are sometimes found preserved in ice in northern Siberia

tide-rip: rough water caused by opposing tides

score: the written composition of a piece of music

jig: a merry dance

Exploring the poem

1. The poem is an invitation to explore a landscape. What kind of landscape does it look at? Support your answer by detailed reference to the text.

2. The poet describes many different animals. Where does he place each of these? Complete the following chart:

Water		Earth			Sky	
Rivers & lakes	Seas & oceans	Below ground	Above ground	Buildings	Dusk	Night
Carp						

3. The only creatures that might belong in the 'Sky' column are the owl, butterfly, flies and sparrows. Which column did you place them in and why?

4. Why do you think the poem focuses on creatures that are in the sea and on the earth?

5. What is the overall setting of the poem? Choose one of the following and support your choice by reference to the poem:
   - a particular time and place
   - several places
   - the universe.

Structure

6. The poem has a very noticeable shape and pattern. It is written in stanzas (see glossary, page 95), but there are separate sections within these.
   - What are these sections about: lines 1–4, 13–16, 25–8, 37–40?
   - What are the other lines about?
   - How does this pattern within the poem reflect its title?

7. What is different about the last seven lines of the poem? Why do you think the poet separates out 'A star falls.' (line 40)?

8. Look closely at the way the words are set out on the page. What does the shape of the poem make you think of?

   Think about the following images from the poem:
   - 'smiles on a nurse' (line 32)
   - 'jaws of a steel vice' (line 28)
   - 'the shaggy world' (line 25)
   - 'a key in a purse' (line 30)

   To what extent does the shape of the poem reflect any or all of these images?

9. The poem uses a lot of rhyme and is strongly repetitive. What does this make you think of? Choose one of the following and give reasons for your choice:
   - a bedtime story
   - a song
   - a prayer
   - something else.

Language

(10) Similes (see glossary, page 95) are a central feature of the language of this poem. They are not difficult to spot because they all use the word 'like'! For example, '...the badger in its bedding' (line 7) is 'Like a loaf in the oven' (line 8). This simile suggests the warmth, security and roundness of the badger, curled up in its lair. Because the bread is baking, it reminds us that although the badger is asleep it is still living and breathing.

Choose another simile about an animal from the poem. What does it make you think of?

(11) Now look at all the similes describing creatures. What do they have in common? What kind of feeling do they suggest, and how do they achieve this effect?

(12) Much of the poem conveys a sense of stillness. How does the poet achieve this? Think about:

- the images he uses
- the effect on time and movement in lines 25–8.

(13) There is also some description of movement in the poem. List the words and phrases that suggest movement.

(14) Look again at the first stanza (see glossary, page 95) of the poem. What does the poet mean by 'all that can no longer feel'? Choose one of the following statements and support your view with evidence from the poem.

- It describes the cold numbness of the living creatures outside.
- The cold in the poem is really a metaphor (see glossary, page 93), an image which describes a shift in the poet's feelings.
- It makes the landscape mythical, like a giant who is numbed by the cold.

(15) The final simile of the poem describes people:

'The sweating farmers
    Turn in their sleep
            Like oxen on spits.' (lines 41–3)

What does this simile suggest?

Writing

1   What kind of world or worlds does the poet describe in **The Warm and the Cold**? Think about:

- how he describes the animals
- how he describes the world around them
- the mood (see glossary, page 94) or atmosphere of the poem
- the structure and shape of the poem.

2   Think of two contrasting aspects of your world, for example, morning/night or work/play. Write a poem based on a collection of similes for each of these.

Tractor

The tractor stands frozen – an agony
To think of. All night
Snow packed its open entrails. Now a head-pincering gale,
A spill of molten ice, smoking snow,
5   Pours into its steel.
At white heat of numbness it stands
In the aimed hosing of ground-level fieriness.

It defies flesh and won't start.
Hands are like wounds already
10   Inside armour gloves, and feet are unbelievable
As if the toe-nails were all just torn off.
I stare at it in hatred. Beyond it
The copse hisses – capitulates miserably
In the fleeing, failing light. Starlings,
15   A dirtier sleetier snow, blow smokily, unendingly, over
Towards plantations Eastward.
All the time the tractor is sinking
Through the degrees, deepening
Into its hell of ice.

20   The starting lever
Cracks its action, like a snapping knuckle.
The battery is alive – but like a lamb
Trying to nudge its solid-frozen mother –
While the seat claims my buttock-bones, bites
25   With the space-cold of earth, which it has joined
In one solid lump.

I squirt commercial sure-fire
Down the black throat – it just coughs.
It ridicules me – a trap of iron stupidity
30 I've stepped into. I drive the battery
As if I were hammering and hammering
The frozen arrangement to pieces with a hammer
And it jabbers laughing pain-crying mockingly
Into happy life.

35 And stands
Shuddering itself full of heat, seeming to enlarge slowly
Like a demon demonstrating
A more-than-usually-complete materialization –
Suddenly it jerks from its solidarity
40 With the concrete, and lurches towards a stanchion
Bursting with superhuman well-being and abandon
Shouting Where Where?

Worse iron is waiting. Power-lift kneels,
Levers awake imprisoned deadweight,
45 Shackle-pins bedded in cast-iron cow-shit.
The blind and vibrating condemned obedience
Of iron to the cruelty of iron,
Wheels screeched out of their night-locks –

Fingers
50 Among the tormented
Tonnage and burning of iron

Eyes
Weeping in the wind of chloroform

And the tractor, streaming with sweat,
55 Raging and trembling and rejoicing.

Explanations

entrails: intestines, guts
copse: a wood
sure-fire: spray designed to get an engine going
jabbers: talks rapidly
stanchion: post used as support
shackle-pins: fasteners

Exploring the poem

1. The poem tells us a kind of story. It has three clear elements to it:
   - the tractor
   - the freezing landscape (or setting)
   - the man and what he is doing.

   Make a chart like the one below:

Tractor	Setting	Man
1	2	9–12
3	3–4	
5–8		

   Decide which lines in the poem refer to each of these elements. Some lines may refer to more than one.
   - Which of the three elements has the most lines in the poem?
   - Which has the fewest?
   - What does this suggest about the poet's memories of his experience?

2. Reread each stanza (see glossary, page 95) carefully. Think about its meaning. For each stanza write one sentence which explains what it is about.

Structure

3. By presenting such powerful images of the tractor, the setting and the man, the poet gives a sort of three-part structure to the poem. However, the distinction between these 'parts' is often blurred. Why do you think he chooses to do this?

4. As the poem develops there are fewer references to the landscape. Why do you think this is?

5. What is the effect of the distinctly different stanza pattern from line 49 to the end of the poem?

Language

6. The poet uses personification (see glossary, page 94) in describing both the tractor and the setting. By giving them human characteristics he makes them seem alive, as in the examples below:

Tractor	Setting
'…All night Snow packed its open entrails.' (lines 2–3)	'…Beyond it The copse hisses – capitulates miserably In the fleeing, failing light' (lines 12–14)
'It defies flesh' (line 8)	

   Find as many other examples as you can of personification.

   In the example above, the copse 'hisses'. This suggests not only the wind and the angry mood of the weather but also the mood of the landscape as it miserably 'capitulates' or accepts defeat. The light flees as though seeking safety.

   Choose two of the examples you have found and explain their effect.

(7) We usually connect feelings with human relationships. However, in this poem, the poet is responding to an environment and a machine. We are made aware of his feelings through his description of the frozen tractor. Find the following lines:

- 'Snow packed its open entrails'
- 'All the time the tractor is sinking'
- 'It ridicules me – a trap of iron stupidity'
- '...seeming to enlarge slowly/Like a demon...'
- 'Shouting Where Where?'
- 'Raging and trembling and rejoicing.'

Explain what they show about the poet's feelings towards the tractor. The first one is done for you.

The tractor	The poet's feelings
'The entrails' describes the exposed engine. The image suggests both agony and numbness, the tractor is like a wounded dead animal.	I think he wants to convey physical pain. He almost seems sorry for the tractor and guilty about it.

(8) In this poem, the poet sometimes borrows images from industry to describe the natural environment.

Look closely at lines 1–6. Pick out the words which suggest industry or industrial processes.

(9) Sound patterns (see glossary, page 95) are important in the poem. Listen to the sound of this line:

'Cracks its action, like a snapping knuckle' (line 21)

'Cracks' is an onomatopoeic word (see glossary, page 94). Its sound helps to suggest what it means. The poet makes a pattern with the sounds which follow: crack – act – snap. We can almost hear the spark or 'crack' of the electricity in the battery. By repeating the sounds, the poet makes us hear the repeated attempts to fire the engine. Note how the simile (see glossary, page 95) used by the poet helps to reinforce this.

(10) Now choose two of the following lines and show how their sound patterns reflect what the words are describing.

- 'A dirtier sleetier snow, blow smokily' (line 15)
- 'hammering and hammering' (line 30)
- 'the fleeing, failing light' (line 14)
- 'cast-iron cow-shit' (line 45)

Assessment objectives

In these activities you have:

• **developed interpretations of texts** e.g. explored the poet's feelings

• **evaluated structural devices** e.g. how the stanza pattern shows the development of feeling

• **evaluated linguistic devices** e.g. how sound patterns and images help to suggest his feelings.

Writing

1 **Tractor** presents a complex picture of a piece of machinery and a man who is trying to get it started. Write about:
   - the ways the tractor is portrayed
   - the feelings the man has towards it.

2 Write a description of a place where you encountered some extreme weather conditions. Use images and sound patterns to give the reader a vivid impression of the place.

Wind

This house has been far out at sea all night,
The woods crashing through darkness, the booming hills,
Winds stampeding the fields under the window
Floundering black astride and blinding wet

5   Till day rose; then under an orange sky
The hills had new places, and wind wielded
Blade-light, luminous black and emerald,
Flexing like the lens of a mad eye.

At noon I scaled along the house-side as far as
10 The coal-house door. Once I looked up –
Through the brunt wind that dented the balls of my eyes
The tent of the hills drummed and strained its guyrope,

The fields quivering, the skyline a grimace,
At any second to bang and vanish with a flap:
15 The wind flung a magpie away and a black-
Back gull bent like an iron bar slowly. The house

Rang like some fine green goblet in the note
That any second would shatter it. Now deep
In chairs, in front of the great fire, we grip
20 Our hearts and cannot entertain book, thought,

Or each other. We watch the fire blazing,
And feel the roots of the house move, but sit on,
Seeing the window tremble to come in,
Hearing the stones cry out under the horizons.

Explanations

brunt: the main force of a blow. Normally a noun
goblet: a large drinking cup/glass
entertain: hold in the mind

Exploring the poem

(1) Every stanza (see glossary, page 95) in the poem tells you something about the force of the wind at different stages of the day, and how it affects what is heard, seen and felt.

Read the first four stanzas and pick out the words which best convey the force of the wind.

(2) The third and fourth stanzas describe the poet in the middle of the day going out into the wind. What does he feel is going to happen to the hills?

(3) The final two stanzas describe being indoors as the wind is raging outside. What are the feelings of the people in the house?

(4) How does the poet feel about the wind? Choose the word or words below that best describe his feelings and explain your choice:
- fear • awe • fascination • hatred.

Structure

(5) What similarities can you see in the structure of the stanzas? Think about
- the number of lines
- the length of line
- the use of rhyme (see glossary, page 95).

(6) Which statement best explains the poem's very strict line and stanza structure?
- There are six stanzas and the poet has six things to say about the wind.
- The poet is imposing a kind of order on a force of nature.
- The poem is written in the shelter of the house, which allows the poet to think in an ordered way about his experience.

(7) The poem is written in six sentences which do not match the six stanzas. The first and third sentences are especially long. What is the effect of these?

(8) Can you see anything unusual about the use of rhyme in this poem?

Language

(9) Explain how each of the following images helps to create a sense of the wind's power.
- 'This house has been far out at sea all night,' (line 1)
- 'Winds stampeding the fields' (line 2)
- 'At noon I scaled along the house-side' (line 9)
- 'The tent of the hills drummed and strained its guyrope,' (line 12)
- '…a black- / Back gull bent like an iron bar' (lines 15–16)
- 'The house / Rang like some fine green goblet' (lines 16–17).

Writing

How does the poet make a natural phenomenon like wind seem interesting? Think about:
- what he has to say about the wind
- the ways he uses language to describe it
- the structure of the poem.

Hawk Roosting

I sit in the top of the wood, my eyes closed.
Inaction, no falsifying dream
Between my hooked head and hooked feet:
Or in sleep rehearse perfect kills and eat.

5   The convenience of the high trees!
The air's buoyancy and the sun's ray
Are of advantage to me;
And the earth's face upward for my inspection.

My feet are locked upon the rough bark.
10   It took the whole of Creation
To produce my foot, my each feather:
Now I hold Creation in my foot

Or fly up, and revolve it all slowly –
I kill where I please because it is all mine.
15   There is no sophistry in my body:
My manners are tearing off heads –

The allotment of death.
For the one path of my flight is direct
Through the bones of the living.
20   No arguments assert my right:

The sun is behind me.
Nothing has changed since I began.
My eye has permitted no change.
I am going to keep things like this.

Explanations

buoyancy: the ability to float
sophistry: argument that seems reasonable
but is actually misleading
allotment: distribution, sharing out

Exploring the poem

① The speaker in this poem is the hawk. What are your first impressions of this bird?

② The poet imagines some thoughts the hawk has. Explore these thoughts, using a table like this.

Thoughts about	Reference	Interpretation
the trees, the wood	lines 1, 5 and 9	The hawk feels that it is above everything else. It can see everything. It is as though the world was made for the hawk's convenience.
the sun	lines 6 and 21	
killing	lines 4, 14–17, 18–19	

③ Look carefully at lines 2 and 3. Why is a dream described as 'falsifying'? What is it that a 'dream' might make false?

④ The poem ends with the phrase 'like this'. What does the hawk mean?

⑤ Try to find evidence from the poem for each of the following statements:

- the hawk is cruel   • the hawk is perfect   • the hawk is admirable
- the hawk is arrogant   • the hawk is single-minded.

For which two is there most evidence?

Structure

⑥ The poet has chosen to write the poem from the hawk's point of view. What is the effect of this? Think about:

- the point the poet is making about the hawk's place in nature
- why point of view is important in this poem.

Language

⑦ The poet captures the voice and character of the hawk. How is this achieved? Think about:

- the effect of the exclamation mark at the end of line 5 on the way you would read the line aloud
- the repetition of 'my' and 'me' in lines 7–12
- the effect of the unusual word order in 'my each feather' (line 11).

Writing

1 What view of a hawk is presented in the poem? Consider the following:

- the poet's feelings about the hawk and its place in nature
- the language the poet uses to describe the hawk.

2 Choose an animal that might be prey for the hawk – a mouse or vole, for example – and write a poem in which you explore its feelings about the hawk and about being hunted.

The poems together

Interpretation

Hawk Roosting and The Warm and the Cold

Both **Hawk Roosting** and **The Warm and the Cold** explore the relationship between creatures and their habitats.

1   Which aspects of **Hawk Roosting** give a sense of the hawk's domination of its world?

2   Which aspects of **The Warm and the Cold** give a sense of creatures at the mercy of the weather and the universe?

3   In what ways does the poet suggest that, in spite of the weather, the creatures in **The Warm and the Cold**, like the hawk, are secure in their immediate environments?

Tractor, Wind and Work and Play

Tractor and **Wind** present people in a battle with their environments. **Work and Play** suggests that winning the battle does not necessarily mean that you win the war.

4   In what ways does **Tractor** show the poet battling against the weather?

5   To what extent does the poet see the tractor as the enemy?

6   In what ways does **Wind** present nature as an irresistible force?

7   **Work and Play** seems to present people and nature in opposition.
   - Which side is winning and which losing?
   - How does the poem show this?

Language

Tractor and Hawk Roosting

Hawk Roosting stands out from the other poems in this section because of its lack of imagery. An example of personification (see glossary, page 94) can be found in 'the earth's face upwards for my inspection' (line 8), but the image is not developed or sustained.

1 Why does the poet give us so little description of the world that the hawk lives in?

2 How many examples of personification can you find in **Tractor**? What do these examples suggest to you about the poet's feelings towards the tractor?

3 The hawk in **Hawk Roosting** and the man in **Tractor** relate differently to their environments. How does the poet's use of personification in **Tractor** help to suggest these differences?

Tractor and Work and Play

Tractor and **Work and Play** suggest the poet's interest in the contrast between nature and the products of the industrial world. These concerns seem to be reflected in his use of metaphor (see glossary, page 93).

4 With what does the poet compare the brutality of the snow and the cold in the first few lines of **Tractor**? Why do you think he chooses these images, and how effective are they?

5 The poet describes the holiday traffic in **Work and Play** as a serpent, an image from nature. How effective is this in expressing how he feels about the cars and the traffic?

6 Can you find a metaphor in **Work and Play** which compares something from nature with an industrial image? How effective is this image?

7 The poet's imagery suggests a fascination with opposites. Why do you think he uses such contrasting images?

Structure

Work and Play and The Warm and the Cold

The structure of **The Warm and The Cold** and **Work and Play** reinforces the idea that the poet is fascinated by contrasts and opposites, but these poems also make powerful use of rhythm and rhyme.

1 Write about the contrasting effects of rhythm in **The Warm and the Cold** and **Work and Play**. What mood does the rhythm bring to these poems? Consider each poem separately.

2 For most of **The Warm and the Cold** the stanza pattern describing the night sky and the creatures stays constant. The number of lines for each contrasting element of the poem remains the same. However, in **Work and Play** the number of lines describing people and cars steadily increases.

   • What do these aspects of the poems suggest to you about the poet's feelings about nature, people and industry?

   • Does the structure of these poems suggest a message to you?

Sample questions

When examiners write questions, they are giving you opportunities to meet specific **assessment objectives**. Before you answer any of the questions on this page, look at question 1 below and the model answer plan opposite.

In the examination you have only 30 minutes to answer the question so you have to decide quickly which poems to focus on. The model answer plan is structured in a way which helps you understand and address clearly the key assessment objectives on which the question is focused:

- interpretation
- language
- structure

---

make cross-references

1   Several of Ted Hughes's poems feature extreme weather. Write about how he conveys his feelings about weather in *two* of the poems.

You should consider:

develop and sustain an interpretation

- his *attitude* to the weather

understand and evaluate linguistic devices

- how he uses language in *interesting* ways to describe the weather

understand and evaluate structural devices

- *how the poems are set out*

read with engagement

- *your own response to what he writes.*

---

2   Write about how the poet uses contrast in **Work and Play** and **The Warm and the Cold**. You should consider:

- the ideas he develops
- how the poems are set out
- the language he uses.

3   Ted Hughes expresses strong feelings in these poems. Choose **two** poems in which you feel he expresses his feelings particularly effectively, giving your reasons. You should write about:

- ideas and feelings
- language
- structure
- your personal response.

4   Write about the different ways in which Ted Hughes explores the world of nature in his poetry.

5   Write about how **Tractor** and **Wind** show people struggling with their environment. You should write about:

- the poet's ideas about the struggle
- the ways he uses language
- how the poems are set out
- your own response.

Model answer plan

1 Several of Ted Hughes's poems feature extreme weather. Write about how he conveys his feelings about weather in **two** of the poems.

You should consider:

- his attitude to the weather
- how he uses language in interesting ways to describe the weather
- how the poems are set out
- your own response to what he writes.

Plan	Examiner's observations
Tractor What is the extreme weather and how does it affect the person in the poem? Focus on the feelings of pain and on what the weather does to the tractor.	You need to respond quickly to the focus of the question, i.e. feelings about the weather.
Move on to look at interesting uses of language: how phrases like 'head-pincering' (line 3), 'hell of ice' (line 18) convey the extreme nature of the weather; the effect of alliteration in '...the seat claims my buttock-bones, bites' (line 24) and 'Weeping in the wind' (line 53); the down-to-earth harshness of 'cast-iron cow-shit' (line 45) etc.	Writing about interesting uses of language is one of the bullet points in the question which you need to address. Avoid the 'spot the image' approach: try to show how the use of language makes the meaning clearer.
You could end your look at this poem by pointing out those details with which you most closely identify. Perhaps you have tried to mend something in the cold and experienced the pain of freezing fingers.	Reading with engagement is an assessment objective. Make sure you don't move away from the poem into writing generally about weather.
Wind Discuss what the extreme weather is in this case and how there are different views of it as the poem develops: its violence; how it changes the way we see the landscape; how it affects those sheltering from its force.	Once again, establish that your response is focused on key words in the question. You may wish to point out that this poem involves a different kind of weather.
Go on to look at the poet's use of language: he selects words for their sounds and for the way they suggest movement and force; he uses a series of interesting metaphors and similes; he uses contrasts of vocabulary to move from sound to sight, from outside to inside.	In looking at a poem like this, which is rich in 'interesting' descriptive language, you will have to be selective – in 30 minutes you can't look at everything.
You may wish to comment on particular details to which you can relate: being inside when a storm is raging outside perhaps; the aptness of images like the one describing the gull.	Writing about your own response is another opportunity to reveal your understanding of the poem.

Poems from Other Cultures and Traditions

The ten poems in this section of the **Anthology** are written by poets from many countries and often reflect the cultures and traditions of those countries. It will help you in your approach to these poems if you have a clear idea of what is meant by 'culture' and 'tradition'.

Culture
Culture is a word you will probably have heard, perhaps in expressions like 'youth culture' or 'working class culture'. It refers to the whole range of history, language, way of life, values and knowledge shared by a particular group or society. It is important to realize that there can be several cultures within one larger culture or society; for example, people from many different cultures live in the United Kingdom.

Tradition
A tradition is an aspect of culture. It is a belief or custom which is handed down within a group from one generation to the next. For example, a tradition might involve eating a particular kind of food on a certain day, or fasting, exchanging gifts, setting off fireworks or lighting candles at a particular time of year. All cultures have their own traditions, which are an essential part of their common history and way of life.

Approaching the poems
When you start to read and study these poems there is no need to adopt a new approach. In the examination you will be tested on the same Assessment Objectives as in Part 1. Clearly, though, in order to respond to the poems and answer the examination questions you need to understand the cultural background. This will help you to a clearer understanding of the similarities and differences between the poems. It will develop your awareness of how poems such as **Search For My Tongue**, **Half-Caste** and **Unrelated Incidents**, explore the question of language, either the experience of having two different languages or of speaking non-standard English, and how **Presents from my Aunts in Pakistan** and **Hurricane Hits England** reflect on people's experience of living in one culture but having roots in another. **Charlotte O'Neil's Song** and **Nothing's Changed** are widely separated from each other by time and distance – one is about a nineteenth-century English emigrant, the other about the experience of being black and poor in 1990s South Africa – but both are powerful protests against poverty and injustice.

As well as enabling you to see stronger links between poems, your knowledge and understanding of a poem's cultural context will help you to a greater understanding of its meaning, structure and language. In the examination, a question may invite you, in some way, to demonstrate your awareness of a poem's cultural context. On the next page you will find the poem **Nothing's Changed** by Tatamkhulu Afrika (also on page 80). The notes next to it show you how that awareness of cultural context can lead you to a better understanding of the meaning, structure and language of the poem.

> What do you learn about the place and its people from **Nothing's Changed**?

Sample approach to a cultural context question

Nothing's Changed

Small round hard stones click
under my heels,
seeding grasses thrust
bearded seeds
5   into trouser cuffs, cans,
trodden on, crunch
in tall, purple-flowering,
amiable weeds.

District Six.
10 No board says it is:
but my feet know,
and my hands,
and the skin about my bones,
and the soft labouring of my lungs,
15 and the hot, white, inwards turning
anger of my eyes.

Brash with glass,
name flaring like a flag,
it squats
20 in the grass and weeds,
incipient Port Jackson trees:
new, up-market, haute cuisine,
guard at the gatepost,
whites only inn.

25 No sign says it is:
but we know where we belong.

I press my nose
to the clear panes, know,
before I see them, there will be
30 crushed ice white glass,
linen falls,
the single rose.

Down the road,
working man's cafe sells
35 bunny chows.
Take it with you, eat
it at a plastic table's top,
wipe your fingers on your jeans,
spit a little on the floor:
40 it's in the bone.

I back from the glass,
boy again,
leaving small mean O
of small, mean mouth.
45 Hands burn
for a stone, a bomb,
to shiver down the glass.
Nothing's changed.   *Tatamkhulu Afrika*

What do you learn about the place and its people from Nothing's Changed?

At first, this poem may not seem to belong to any particular 'culture'. The language is standard English and the stones, grasses, cans and 'tall, purple-flowering, amiable weeds' could be anywhere. The mood of this stanza is calm, even neutral.

We learn that this place has a name – it is District Six, which sounds faceless, bureaucratic, even slightly disturbing. This is the first hint that the poem is set somewhere other than Britain. We also learn that the man in the poem has known it well in the past:

'…my feet know, / and my hands, / and the skin about my bones.'

At this point the mood of the poem changes to one of rising anger.

The references to Port Jackson in line 21 and to the 'whites only inn' in line 24 suggest that the setting is a society divided along racial lines, most probably South Africa. Until 1994, the political system known as apartheid (which means 'separate development') meant that black people were not allowed to mix socially with whites, travel on the same buses or even live in the same areas. The best things were labelled 'whites only' – reserved exclusively for white people. The harsh sounds of the language used to describe the inn:

'Brash with glass, / name flaring like a flag, / it squats.' (lines 17–19)

help to reinforce the sense of the man's rage.

Lines 25–6 are the turning-point of the poem and help to explain the man's anger.

'No sign says it is' (line 25)

echoes 'No board says it is' in line 10 and tells us that, although apartheid has been officially abolished, nothing has really changed. The inn is still effectively 'whites only'; the man knows that he would not be welcome there because he is black and poor –

'but we know where we belong' (line 26) –

and that the 'guard at the gatepost' would turn him back if he tried to go in.

The voice of the poem is one of great anger and bitterness. It is a protest against a society where the majority of the population are still powerless and excluded because of their skin colour. This exclusion seems to be symbolized by the glass which is mentioned repeatedly throughout the poem; the man is always on the outside, looking through glass at the good life which he wants but cannot have. The final stanza hints at an explosion of violence if the situation is allowed to continue:

'Hands burn
For a stone, a bomb,
To shiver down the glass' (lines 45–7)

but seems to hold out no hope of any real improvement — 'Nothing's changed'.

Sujata Bhatt

from Search For My Tongue

You ask me what I mean
by saying I have lost my tongue.
I ask you, what would you do
if you had two tongues in your mouth,
5 and lost the first one, the mother tongue,
and could not really know the other,
the foreign tongue.
You could not use them both together
even if you thought that way.
10 And if you lived in a place you had to
speak a foreign tongue,
your mother tongue would rot,
rot and die in your mouth
until you had to spit it out.
15 I thought I spit it out
but overnight while I dream,

મને હતું કે આખ્ખી જીભ આખ્ખી ભાષા,
(munay hutoo kay aakhee jeebh aakhee bhasha)

મેં થૂંકી નાખી છે.
20 (may thoonky nakhi chay)

પરંતુ રાત્રે સ્વપ્નમાં મારી ભાષા પાછી આવે છે.
(parantoo rattray svupnama mari bhasha pachi aavay chay)

ફૂલની જેમ મારી ભાષા મારી જીભ
(foolnee jaim mari bhasha mari jeebh)

25 મોઢામાં ખીલે છે.
(modhama kheelay chay)

ફૂલની જેમ મારી ભાષા મારી જીભ
(fullnee jaim mari bhasha mari jeebh)

મોઢામાં પાકે છે.
30 (modhama pakay chay)
it grows back, a stump of a shoot
grows longer, grows moist, grows strong
veins,
it ties the other tongue in knots,
35 the bud opens, the bud opens in my mouth,
it pushes the other tongue aside.
Everytime I think I've forgotten,
I think I've lost the mother tongue,
it blossoms out of my mouth.

Explanations

mother tongue:
your native or
original language.
It can also mean
the language from
which another
language has
developed, as a
mother gives birth

Exploring the poem

(1) The poem seems to fall into three sections: lines 1–16, 17–30 and 31–8. But you will notice that the sense of line 16 flows into line 31.

The poet has told someone 'I have lost my tongue' (line 2) and the poem explains what she means.

- What reasons does the poet give in lines 1–16 for having lost her 'mother tongue'?
- Now read lines 31–8. What else are we told about her 'mother tongue'?

(2) Look at the middle section in Gujerati.

- Why do you think the poet included this?
- Why do you think it is written in the original script with the phonetic presentation (see glossary, page 94) in brackets afterwards?

(3) The section in Gujerati (lines 17–30), when translated into English, means much the same as lines 15–16 and 31–8. Do you think it matters whether you can translate the Gujerati or not?

Structure

(4) Why has the poet included the Gujerati section in the middle of an English sentence? Is there anything in the rest of the poem to give you a clue?

Language

The poet develops her idea by using an extended metaphor (see glossary, page 93); she compares her 'tongue' to a plant.

(5) In what ways is the poet's original language like a plant?

(6) How does the extended metaphor help you to understand the poet's point of view about her original language?

(7) What differences can you see between the way language is used in the first section (lines 1–16) and in the last section (lines 31–8)?

(8) Why, in line 37, does the poet use the phrase '*the* mother tongue' instead of '*my* mother tongue'?

Culture

(9) What does this poem say about the importance of language to a culture? To what extent does it highlight the difficulties of being part of two cultures?

Sujata Bhatt was born in India in 1956. Her family moved to the US in the 1960s and she now lives in Germany. Some of the poems in her first book, **Brunizem,** *are written both in English and Gujerati, her mother tongue. In particular the long poem* **Search For My Tongue** *contains a translation of the Gujerati within the text.* **Brunizem** *won the Commonwealth Poetry Prize in 1988. A volume of selected poems was published by Carcanet in 1997.*

Assessment objectives

In these activities you have:

- **developed interpretations of texts** e.g. explored the poet's feelings about her two languages
- **evaluated structural devices** e.g. the effect of 'interrupting' the English words with Gujerati
- **evaluated linguistic devices** e.g. the effect of the different languages in the poem.

Writing

1 How is the poet's attitude towards her 'mother tongue' developed in the poem? Write about:

- her feelings about her original language, Gujerati
- interesting features of the language she uses in the poem
- how the shape of the poem helps her present her feelings.

2 If, like Sujata Bhatt, you have a mother tongue which is not English, write about your experience of moving between two languages.

Tom Leonard

from **Unrelated Incidents**

	this is thi
	six a clock
	news thi
	man said n
5	thi reason
	a talk wia
	BBC accent
	iz coz yi
	widny wahnt
10	mi ti talk
	aboot thi
	trooth wia
	voice lik
	wanna yoo
15	scruff. if
	a toktaboot
	thi trooth
	lik wanna yoo
	scruff yi
20	widny thingk
	it wuz troo.
	jist wonna yoo
	scruff tokn.
	thirza right
25	way ti spell
	ana right way
	ti tok it. this
	is me tokn yir
	right way a
30	spellin. this
	is ma trooth.
	yooz doant no
	thi trooth
	yirsellz cawz
35	yi canny talk
	right. this is
	the six a clock
	nyooz. belt up.

Explanations

BBC accent: also known as Standard English or Received Pronunciation, this is the 'correct', unaccented English used by news presenters and others in positions of authority. It is often thought of as conferring credibility and status because it reveals nothing of the speaker's place of origin or social background

Exploring the poem

Tom Leonard was born in Scotland in 1944 and writes mainly in Glasgow dialect. He has been writing for thirty years, and his collected works, which mix dialect poems with controversial essays, are published by Vintage. The sequence **Unrelated Incidents** *is included in* **Intimate Voices: Selected Works 1965–1983**.

(1) This poem, written in Scots dialect (see glossary, page 93), can be seen as a humorous comment on people's attitudes towards regional accents and the arguments over 'standard' and 'non-standard' English. The words in the poem have been spelt out phonetically (see glossary, page 94) instead of in the 'correct' way so that they reflect the Glasgow accent of the speaker.

Find the Glaswegian versions of the following words in the poem and write down any differences in the spelling of each word.
- the • news • and • I • talk • with • because • you
- wouldn't • one • about • truth • yourselves

(2) Now use the words above to help you rewrite the poem as precisely as possible in standard English. Set out your version, as far as you can, in the same form, i.e. with the same line lengths as the poem. Try to express the ideas clearly.

(3) What ideas are expressed in the poem about:
- non-standard English • accents • the television audience • the news?

Structure

(4) The poem has unusually short line lengths. Does this make you take it less seriously?

(5) Try reading the poem out loud (in your best BBC accent) and ensure that you pause carefully at the end of every line. What is the effect of this?

Language

(6) Put the following statements in an order which shows the features of the poem that cause you the most difficulty and which cause you the least.
- **a** phonetic spellings
- **b** absence of punctuation
- **c** the way the words are put together
- **d** the words used
- **e** the way the argument develops
- **f** the ideas being expressed.

(7) Which version of the poem makes the best sense to you: the dialect version, your standard English version, both or neither? Explain why.

Culture

(8) The poem highlights the fact that even in a small country like Britain, there are many variations in speech and accent. Is this an attractive feature of a country, or should we all speak a 'standard' version of the language?

Writing

1 What is the poet saying about attitudes to dialect and standard forms of English?

2 Write a short poem making a serious point in a humorous way.

Half-Caste

Excuse me
standing on one leg
I'm half-caste

Explain yuself
5   wha yu mean
when yu say half-caste
yu mean when picasso
mix red an green
is a half-caste canvas/
10   explain yuself
wha yu mean
when yu say half-caste
yu mean when light an shadow
mix in de sky
15   is a half-caste weather/
well in dat case
england weather
nearly always half-caste
in fact some o dem cloud
20   half-caste till dem overcast
so spiteful dem dont want de sun pass
ah rass/
explain yuself
wha yu mean
25   when yu say half-caste
yu mean tchaikovsky
sit down at dah piano
an mix a black key
wid a white key
30   is a half-caste symphony/

Girl before a Mirror/Pablo Picasso © Succession Picasso/DACS 1998

Explain yuself
wha yu mean
Ah listening to yu wid de keen
half of mih ear
35   Ah lookin at yu wid de keen
half of mih eye
and when I'm introduced to yu

I'm sure you'll understand
why I offer yu half-a-hand
40   an when I sleep at night
I close half-a-eye
consequently when I dream
I dream half-a-dream
an when moon begin to glow
45   I half-caste human being
cast half-a-shadow
but yu must come back tomorrow

wid de whole of yu eye
an de whole of yu ear
50   an de whole of yu mind

an I will tell yu
de other half
of my story

Explanations

half-caste: a term used to describe people born of parents of different colour. Once in common usage, it is now considered insulting
picasso: Pablo Picasso, a Spanish artist famous for some of the most influential paintings of the twentieth century
ah rass: an expression of disgust
tchaikovsky: Peter Tchaikovsky, a famous nineteenth-century Russian composer

Exploring the poem

John Agard was born in Guyana and moved to Britain in 1977. He has written poetry for both adults and children and enjoys performing his work. His earlier poetry can be found in **Mangoes and Bullets** *(published by Serpent's Tail). He has recently published* **From the Devil's Pulpit** *(Bloodaxe), a devil's eye view of the world. He was the first Poet in Residence at the BBC, a post which he held from January–June 1998.*

(1) Look at the first 30 lines. How does the poet use the following examples to make the reader think about the term 'half-caste'?

- Picasso   • the English weather   • Tchaikovsky.

(2) Lines 4–30 are focused on things that are mixed. How does the poet shift the focus in lines 33–46?

(3) What is the poet really saying in lines 47–50?

Structure

(4) The poem is divided into five stanzas (see glossary, page 95). Why do you think the poet left a gap between lines 37 and 38, and between 50 and 51, when the sense of the lines seems to run on?

(5) How many examples of repetition can you find? What is its effect?

(6) The sounds of words help establish the rhythms (see glossary, page 95) of the poem. Reread lines 4–9. Apart from the repetition you will also hear the rhyme (see glossary, page 95) of 'mean' and 'green' and the echo of 'half-caste' in 'canvas'. Find another section of the poem in which the sounds of words seem especially important to the rhythm, and explain why.

Language

(7) How does the poet make his poem seem conversational?

(8) What are the main features of the poet's language which make it different from standard English?

Oral work

(9) This is a poem that needs to be read aloud. It is written in Caribbean dialect (see glossary, page 93). Working through some of these activities should help you think about the kind of tone in which to read it.

Make a copy of the poem to use as a working script which can be underlined and highlighted. Before reading it aloud, think carefully about the tone of voice you will use. Will you sound:

- angry   • sarcastic   • contemptuous   • good-humoured   • exasperated?

How will you treat the constant repetition? Where will you pause and use emphasis?

Culture

(10) Would you say that the poem is mainly directed against white people who use the term 'half-caste'? Support your answer with evidence from the text.

Writing

What is the poet's attitude towards:

- the term 'half-caste'
- the people who use the term?

Blessing

The skin cracks like a pod.
There never is enough water.

Imagine the drip of it,
the small splash, echo
5 in a tin mug,
the voice of a kindly god.

Sometimes, the sudden rush
of fortune. The municipal pipe bursts,
silver crashes to the ground
10 and the flow has found
a roar of tongues. From the huts,
a congregation: every man woman
child for streets around
butts in, with pots,
15 brass, copper, aluminium,
plastic buckets,
frantic hands,

and naked children
screaming in the liquid sun,
20 their highlights polished to perfection,
flashing light,
as the blessing sings
over their small bones.

Explanations

Blessing: something
precious, given rather
than earned; a free gift
fortune: wealth, good
luck or fate
municipal: public,
belonging to the town
tongues: voices
congregation: a group
of people assembled
together for a common
purpose

Exploring the poem

*Imtiaz Dharker was born in Pakistan in 1954 and now lives in Bombay, where she works as an artist and film-maker. Her two books of poetry, **Purdah** (1989) and **Postcards from God** (1994) have recently been published in one volume by Bloodaxe Books.*

(1) On first reading the poem the 'burst' waterpipe seems to be cause for celebration. But you need to think carefully whether this is really the case.
- What does the poet describe in the first 6 lines?
- To what does the phrase 'the sudden rush of fortune' (lines 7–8) refer?
- How do the people respond to the burst pipe?
- What is described in the final stanza (see glossary, page 95) of the poem?

(2) Look carefully at stanzas three and four. Does the poem distinguish between the responses of the adults and the children? If so, how?

Language

(3) What is the effect of the simile (see glossary, page 95) 'The skin cracks like a pod' in the first line?

(4) Think about the directness of the statement: 'There never is enough water'. Think about how you might read lines 3–6 aloud. How does the poet get the reader to imagine 'the drip' of water?

(5) The opening six lines are very simple and straightforward compared with the 'bustle' of the lines that follow. How does the poet create an atmosphere of noise and activity here? Give examples of particular words and phrases.

(6) Explain the meanings of the following images (see glossary, page 93) and comment on their effectiveness:
- 'silver crashes to the ground' (line 9)   • 'frantic hands' (line 17)
- 'the liquid sun' (line 19)
- 'highlights polished to perfection' (line 20)
- 'the blessing sings' (line 22).

Structure

(7) Think about the way the poem is divided up. Write a short summary of each stanza to show how the poet develops her ideas.

(8) Look at the length of the sentences. Why do you think the poet conveys some ideas in very short sentences and some ideas in very long ones?

(9) What do you notice about the rhyme scheme (see glossary, page 95)? Find examples of words that rhyme and suggest reasons for the choices the poet has made.

(10) Read the first and last lines of the poem together. What is the effect of these two lines when combined in this way?

Culture

(11) What do you learn about the place and its people from this poem?

(12) There are several references suggestive of religion in the poem:
- 'a kindly god'   • 'a congregation'   • 'the blessing sings'.

But there is nothing to suggest any particular religion. Why?

Writing

How does the poet convey to the reader a sense of the importance of water to this community?

Assessment objectives

In these activities you have:
- **developed interpretations of texts** e.g. what the water means to the people in the poem
- **evaluated linguistic devices** e.g. how the images suggest the importance of water
- **evaluated structural devices** e.g. how the beginning and end of the poem makes its mood ambiguous.

Presents from my Aunts in Pakistan

They sent me a salwar kameez
      peacock-blue,
         and another
    glistening like an orange split open,
5 embossed slippers, gold and black
      points curling.
    Candy-striped glass bangles
      snapped, drew blood.
    Like at school, fashions changed
10   in Pakistan –
the salwar bottoms were broad and stiff,
      then narrow.
My aunts chose an apple-green sari,
    silver-bordered
15   for my teens.

I tried each satin-silken top –
    was alien in the sitting-room.
I could never be as lovely
      as those clothes –
20   I longed
for denim and corduroy.
    My costume clung to me
      and I was aflame,
I couldn't rise up out of its fire,
25   half-English,
      unlike Aunt Jamila.

I wanted my parents' camel-skin lamp –
    switching it on in my bedroom,
to consider the cruelty
30   and the transformation
from camel to shade,
    marvel at the colours
      like stained glass.

My mother cherished her jewellery –
35   Indian gold, dangling, filigree,
      But it was stolen from our car.
The presents were radiant in my wardrobe.
    My aunts requested cardigans
      from Marks and Spencers.

My salwar kameez
40   didn't impress the schoolfriend
who sat on my bed, asked to see
    my weekend clothes.
But often I admired the mirror-work,
    tried to glimpse myself
45   in the miniature
glass circles, recall the story
    how the three of us
      sailed to England.
Prickly heat had me screaming on the way.
50   I ended up in a cot
in my English grandmother's dining-room,
    found myself alone,
      playing with a tin boat.

I pictured my birthplace
55   from fifties' photographs.
      When I was older
there was conflict, a fractured land
    throbbing through newsprint.
Sometimes I saw Lahore –
60   my aunts in shaded rooms,
screened from male visitors,
    sorting presents,
      wrapping them in tissue.

Or there were beggars, sweeper-girls
65   and I was there –
      of no fixed nationality,
staring through fretwork
      at the Shalimar Gardens.

Explanations

salwar kameez: salwar = loose trousers traditionally worn in Pakistan and Bangladesh; kameez = the loose shirt worn over the top of the salwar

embossed: with a raised pattern

sari: the traditional dress of women of India and some parts of Pakistan

filigree: delicate metalwork made from twisted gold or silver wire

radiant: bright

Prickly heat: a severe itching of the skin caused by heat

Lahore: capital of Punjab province and the second largest city in Pakistan

fretwork: decorative carving

Shalimar Gardens: gardens in Lahore, famous for their beauty

Exploring the poem

Moniza Alvi was born in Pakistan in 1954 and moved to Britain when she was a child. She worked as an English teacher in London and edited the **Poetry London Newsletter**. *Her poetry can be found in* **The Country at my Shoulder** *(Oxford University Press, 1993) and* **A Bowl of Warm Air** *(Oxford University Press, 1996).*

(1) Two cultures are contrasted in this poem. Several objects from the culture of Pakistan cross over into the girl's world in England.

Identify these objects. How does the girl respond to them?

The objects from Pakistan	Response
clothes: salwar kameez, slippers	gorgeous but too exotic – 'alien in the sitting room'

(2) What is the difference between the 'denim and corduroy', the 'cardigans from Marks and Spencers' and the clothes the aunts send?

(3) What memories does the girl have of her journey to England?

(4) What view of Pakistan does the girl get from photographs and newspapers? In what ways does life for her aunts seem different from life in England?

(5) Discuss the following statements, supporting your point of view with evidence from the poem.

- the girl regrets ever leaving Pakistan
- the girl feels sad that she has lost her Pakistani identity
- the poem is a search for a true identity.

Structure

(6) The poem is written in free verse, which means the lines are of different lengths and there is no rhyme scheme (see glossary, page 95).

The poem is organized into seven stanzas. Write a short summary of each stanza to show the development of the ideas. The first one is done for you:

Stanza 1: describes the beautifully coloured clothes sent to the girl. She shows that what is fashionable in Pakistan changes just as it does in England.

Language

(7) List words and phrases from the poem that suggest the following characteristics of Pakistani culture:

- exotic • colourful • mysterious.

Culture

(8) Explore the differences between the two cultures described by this poem. Think about the ways of life as well as objects.

Writing

What does this poem have to say about living in one culture but having roots in another?

Assessment objectives

In these activities you have:

• **developed interpretations of texts** e.g. explored the writer's feelings of being 'half-English'

• **evaluated structural devices** e.g. how the poem is organized into stanzas

• **evaluated linguistic devices** e.g. how the writer uses language to emphasize the differences between two cultures.

Ogun

My uncle made chairs, tables, balanced doors on, dug out
coffins, smoothing the white wood out

with plane and quick sandpaper until
it shone like his short-sighted glasses.

5   The knuckles of his hands were sil-
vered knobs of nails hit, hurt and flat-

tened out with blast of heavy hammer. He was knock-knee'd, flat-
footed and his clip clop sandals slapped across the concrete

flooring of his little shop where canefield mulemen and a fleet
10   of Bedford lorry drivers dropped in to scratch themselves and talk.

There was no shock of wood, no beam
of light mahogany his saw teeth couldn't handle.

When shaping squares for locks, a key hole
care tapped rat tat tat upon the handle

15   of his humpbacked chisel. Cold
world of wood caught fire as he whittled: rectangle

window frames, the intersecting x of fold-
ing chairs, triangle

trellises, the donkey
20   box-cart in its squeaking square.

But he was poor and most days he was hungry.
Imported cabinets with mirrors, formica table

tops, spine-curving chairs made up of tubes, with hollow
steel-like bird bones that sat on rubber ploughs,

25   thin beds, stretched not on boards, but blue high-tensioned cables,
were what the world preferred.

And yet he had a block of wood that would have baffled them.
With knife and gimlet care he worked away at this on Sundays,

explored its knotted hurts, cutting his way
30   along its yellow whorls until his hands could feel

how it had swelled and shivered, breathing air,
its weathered green burning to rings of time,

its contoured grain still tuned to roots and water.
And as he cut, he heard the creak of forests:

35 green lizard faces gulped, grey memories with moth
    eyes watched him from their shadows, soft

    liquid tendrils leaked among the flowers
    and a black rigid thunder he had never heard within his hammer

    came stomping up the trunks. And as he worked within his
40   shattered
    Sunday shop, the wood took shape: dry shuttered

    eyes, slack anciently everted lips, flat
    ruined face, eaten by pox, ravaged by rat

    and woodworm, dry cistern mouth, cracked
45 gullet crying for the desert, the heavy black

    enduring jaw; lost pain, lost iron;
    emerging woodwork image of his anger.

Explanations

Ogun: powerful West African god of iron and thunder. Ogun has been an important god in both the tropical and desert regions of West Africa since ancient times

plane: hand tool with a flat surface and protruding blade, used to shave a piece of wood until it is level, smooth and the right thickness

canefield mulemen: men in charge of the mules used to carry sugar cane from the cane fields

shock: hard or difficult part of the wood

whittled: carved, shaved away

trellises: fence or screen made by the criss-crossing of slats of wood

formica: synthetic sheet material

gimlet: hand tool for boring fine holes

whorls: circular patterns

contoured: ringed, as if showing hills or mountains on map

tendrils: slender, leafless plant stems which cling to other plants for support

everted: turned outwards

cistern: water tank

gullet: throat

Exploring the poem

Edward Kamau Brathwaite was born in Barbados in 1930. After winning a scholarship to study history at Cambridge University, he went on to take a PhD in Jamaican history. He then went to Ghana where he taught for several years before returning to the Caribbean to lecture at the University of the West Indies in Jamaica. **Ogun** is taken from a trilogy called **The Arrivants** (Oxford University Press, 1981). Brathwaite has published many books of poetry and is one of the best-known Caribbean poets.

(1) The poet's memories of his uncle are developed in three distinct sections: lines 1–20, lines 21–6 and lines 27–47. Copy out a table, like the one below, and record:

• what each section is about   • the poet's thoughts and feelings.

Lines	The uncle, his work and other things	The poet's thoughts and feelings
1–20	In spite of his knock knees, flat feet and short sight, he was a skilled craftsman and could tackle almost any work involving wood.	These lines show affection. The poet admires his uncle's skill and this is shown in the way he vividly recalls sights and sounds of the workshop.

Language

(2) In lines 1–20 the poet makes clever use of sound patterns (see glossary, page 95), e.g. the repetition of the *sh-* and *s-* sounds in 'it shone like his short-sighted glasses' (line 4) helps to suggest the hissing sound of the plane and the sandpaper.

Try to find other examples of words and lines which capture the different sounds of the workshop. Explain why each of these is effective.

(3) The poet sometimes uses metaphor to describe the uncle and his work, e.g. 'the knuckles of his hands were silver knobs of nails, hit, hurt and flattened...' (lines 5–7).

• Find other examples of lines which describe both the uncle and his work.

• What do these suggest about the uncle and the life he has led?

(4) List the words and phrases used to describe the furniture in lines 21–6. What impression is created of this furniture that 'the world preferred'?

(5) Read lines 27–41. How does the poet create the sense of a journey? What kind of journey is this?

(6) Which words in lines 41–7 convey the 'image of his anger'? Comment on their effectiveness.

Structure

(7) The poem is written mainly in couplets (see glossary, page 93). Sometimes they contain complete sentences and sometimes the sentences are carried on. What effect does this have when you read the poem aloud?

Culture

(8) What is the poet saying about his roots and his culture?

(9) What do you understand by 'the emerging woodwork image of his anger', and where does the anger come from? Do you find this line sad or hopeful? Explain your response.

Writing

Explain what each section of the poem shows us about the poet, his uncle and the poet's feelings towards his uncle.

Fiona Farrell

from **Passengers**

Clara Roskruge, 16. Domestic servant. Cornwall. 'Indian Empire' 1864.
Charlotte O'Neil, 17. General servant. Origin unknown. 'Isabella Hercus' 1871.
Ann James, 33. Laundress. Abergavenny. 'Light Brigade' 1868.
Harriet Attiwell, 20. Domestic servant. Leicestershire. 'Cameo' 1859.
Eliza Lambert, 14. Domestic servant. Surrey. 'Mystery' 1858.
Nineteenth-century ships' records

Charlotte O'Neil's Song

You rang your bell and I answered.
I polished your parquet floor.
I scraped out your grate
and I washed your plate
5   and I scrubbed till my hands were raw.

You lay on a silken pillow.
I lay on an attic cot.
That's the way it should be, you said.
That's the poor girl's lot.
10 You dined at eight
and slept till late.

I emptied your chamber pot.
The rich man earns his castle, you said.
The poor deserve the gate.

15 But I'll never say 'sir'
or 'thank you ma'am'
and I'll never curtsey more.
You can bake your bread
and make your bed
20 and answer your own front door.

I've cleaned your plate
and I've cleaned your house
and I've cleaned the clothes you wore.
But now you're on your own, my dear.
25 I won't be there any more.
And I'll eat when I please
and I'll sleep where I please

and you can open your own front door.

Explanations

'Isabella Hercus': in the nineteenth century, ships like the *Isabella Hercus* took passengers from Britain to a new life in countries like New Zealand or Canada. Here the poet gives a 'voice' to one such passenger
parquet: expensive flooring material made from hardwood blocks
grate: the iron base of an open fireplace
cot: 1 child's bed **2** small, simple bed
chamber pot: bedroom pot

Exploring the poem

Fiona Farrell was born, and still lives, in New Zealand. She writes poems, stories and plays and has published one volume of poetry, **Cutting Out** *(Auckland University Press).* **Charlotte O'Neil's Song** *is from a sequence of four poems called* **Passengers**.

(1) The ship's record tells us very little about Charlotte O'Neil and her background. What does the poem suggest about:

- the place where she worked
- the kind of work she did
- the attitude of her employer
- her reasons for leaving
- the changes she made to her life
- the kind of person Charlotte was?

Structure

(2) The poem can be thought of as an argument. It develops in stages and expresses a strong point of view. In order to present the argument effectively the poet uses contrast and repetition. She uses antithesis or contrasting pairs (see glossary, page 93) to highlight something which is wrong or unjust:

'You lay on a silken pillow
I lay on an attic cot.' (lines 6–7)

and a 'pattern of three' (see glossary, page 94) to hammer the points home:

'I scraped out your grate
and I washed your plate
and I scrubbed till my hands were raw.' (lines 3–5)

Try to find more examples of contrast and repetition. How effective are they?

(3) The poet uses tenses in an interesting way. Which lines refer to:

- the past
- the present
- the future?

Language

(4) The title refers to the poem as a song. It certainly has a very strong rhythm (see glossary, page 95). Try reading it to a regular beat. Tap out the rhythm of the lines as you read them. What effect does this have on individual words and lines?

(5) Would you describe the rhythm as:

- cheerful
- sombre
- upbeat
- slow?

What does the rhythm suggest about how Charlotte sees her future?

Culture

(6) Poems, speeches and songs have often been used to protest about the unjust oppression of one group or culture by another.

Make a class collection of as many of these as you can find.

Writing

1 In what ways can **Charlotte O'Neil's Song** be described as a protest song? Think about:

- what you have learned about her life
- what the poem says about injustice
- the use of contrast and repetition
- the use of rhythm and rhyme (see glossary, page 95).

2 Prepare a speech, a poem or a song on a subject about which you feel strongly. Present this to your group.

An Old Woman

Explanations

paise: an Indian coin. A fifty paise coin is half a rupee. Its English equivalent would be a little less than a penny

horseshoe shrine: a shrine is a place considered holy, dedicated to a god or a saint. People often travel in order to visit a shrine

burr: clinging, hooked seed

farce: absurd or pointless pretence, a comedy

crone: withered old woman

small change: coins of little value

An old woman grabs
hold of your sleeve
and tags along.

She wants a fifty paise coin.
5 She says she will take you
to the horseshoe shrine.

You've seen it already.
She hobbles along anyway
and tightens her grip on your shirt.

10 She won't let you go.
You know how old women are.
They stick to you like a burr.

You turn round and face her
with an air of finality.
15 You want to end the farce.

When you hear her say,
'What else can an old woman do
on hills as wretched as these?'

You look right at the sky.
20 Clear through the bullet holes
she has for her eyes.

And as you look on,
the cracks that begin round her eyes
spread beyond her skin.

25 And the hills crack.
And the temples crack.
And the sky falls

with a plate-glass clatter
round the shatter-proof crone
30 who stands alone.

And you are reduced
to so much small change
in her hand.

Arun Kolatkar

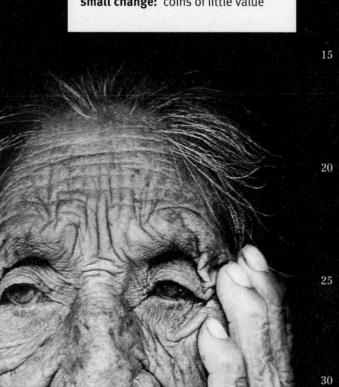

Exploring the poem

Arun Kolatkar was born in India in 1932 and worked as a graphic artist in Bombay. He has published one book of poems in English, **Jejuri** (Clearing House, India), which won the Commonwealth Poetry Prize in 1976.

1. An old woman begs money from a stranger. She offers to take him to a nearby shrine in return.

   Copy out a chart like the one below. What do lines 1–18 tell you about the man's thoughts, feelings and attitude towards the old woman?

Lines	Attitude, thoughts and feelings
7 You've seen it already	Wants her to go away. There's a hint of impatience and boredom with the place and the situation. He might not have spoken directly to her. He keeps on walking.
11 You know how old women are	
12 They stick to you like a burr	

2. What does the old woman say to him? How do her words seem to change the way he sees her?

3. What are his thoughts and feelings in the final stanza (see glossary, page 95) of the poem?

Structure

4. Look at the middle stanza of the poem. What is it about? Why is the use of direct speech important here? How is this stanza central to the meaning of the poem?

5. There are only two lines in the poem that are true rhymes (see glossary, page 95):

   'round the shatter-proof crone
   who stands alone.' (lines 29–30)

   Why has the poet drawn attention to these lines in this way?

Language

6. There is only one image in the first half of the poem:

   'They stick to you like a burr.' (line 12)

   What is suggested by this simile (see glossary, page 95)?

7. As soon as the woman has spoken, the language becomes much richer and the images much stronger. Look again at lines 22–30.
   - What is the poet describing here?
   - What use does he make of repetition? What effect does this have?

Culture

8. What do you think the poet's attitude is towards:
   - people who beg on the streets
   - the people they beg from?

Writing

Assessment objectives

In these activities you have:
- **developed interpretations of texts** e.g. the attitude of the visitor towards the old woman
- **evaluated structural devices** e.g. how the structure of the poem suggests a turning point
- **evaluated linguistic devices** e.g. how the images reflect a change in attitude.

The poem presents a clear sense of 'before' and 'after'. Show how the poet's attitude to the old woman changes in the course of the poem. You should include comment on the structure of the poem and his choice of words.

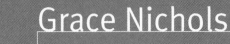
Grace Nichols

Hurricane Hits England

It took a hurricane, to bring her closer
To the landscape.
Half the night she lay awake,
The howling ship of the wind,
5   Its gathering rage,
Like some dark ancestral spectre.

Talk to me Huracan
Talk to me Oya
Talk to me Shango
10   And Hattie,
My sweeping, back-home cousin.

Tell me why you visit
An English coast?
What is the meaning
15   Of old tongues
Reaping havoc
In new places?

The blinding illumination,
Even as you short-
20   Circuit us
Into further darkness?

What is the meaning of trees
Falling heavy as whales
Their crusted roots
25   Their cratered graves?

O why is my heart unchained?

Tropical Oya of the Weather,
I am aligning myself to you,
I am following the movement of your winds,
30   I am riding the mystery of your storm.

Ah, sweet mystery,
Come to break the frozen lake in me,
Shaking the foundations of the very trees within me,
Come to let me know
35   That the earth is the earth is the earth.

Explanations

Hurricane: storms of tropical intensity hit the south of England in 1987 and 1989
ancestral: belonging to our ancestors. Our ancestors are the people from whom we are descended
spectre: ghost
Huracan: a form of the word 'hurricane'
Oya: one of the gods of the Yoruba people of West Africa. Oya is the goddess of wind, a symbol of change
Shango: another god of the Yoruba people, the god of thunder and lightning
Hattie: a famous Caribbean hurricane
aligning: bringing into line, co-ordinating with

Exploring the poem

Grace Nichols was born in Guyana in 1950. After university, she worked in the Caribbean and as a journalist and reporter until she moved to Britain in 1977. She now lives and writes in Sussex. Her first book of poetry was published in 1983, the year she won the Commonwealth Poetry Prize. Grace Nichols also writes novels and compiles poetry anthologies for younger readers. Her poetry celebrates life with a particular warmth. **Hurricane** *is taken from her collection of poetry,* **Sunrise** *(Virago), published in 1996.*

(1) The poem shows the effect of the hurricane on a woman's thoughts. Which details in the opening two stanzas show that the storm brought thoughts of the Caribbean?

(2) The middle section of the poem consist of a series of five questions. What does each one tell you about the woman's thoughts and feelings? Use a chart like the one below to help plan your ideas. The first one is done for you.

Questions	The thoughts and feelings behind the question
Tell me why you visit An English coast? (lines 12-13)	*The woman finds it strange that a kind of tropical storm should hit England; it is very unusual.*

(3) In the final stanza (see glossary, page 95) the woman seems very positive about the storm. Discuss the following statements, finding evidence from the poem to support your point of view:

a The storm has reminded her of her roots and she is grateful for that.

b The storm has brought out something in her which was previously hidden.

c She feels that, like the trees, she has been uprooted from her foundations.

Structure

(4) For most of the poem, the speaker is the woman experiencing the hurricane. Who speaks in the first stanza?

(5) The poem can be broken into three sections: lines 1–6; lines 7–26; and the final two stanzas. Write a short summary of each of these sections.

(6) Why do you think the poet has made line 26 a separate line? What is its effect?

Language

(7) Explore the following images (see glossary, page 93). Why do you think the poet chose them? How effective are they?

- The howling wind gathers rage 'Like some dark ancestral spectre' (line 6)
- Trees uprooted by the wind are 'Falling heavy as whales' (line 23)
- The hurricane breaks 'the frozen lake in me' (line 32).

Culture

(8) The hurricane prompts the poet to reflect on living in England and about her roots. What do you think her feelings are about living in a country different from that of her birth?

Writing

How does the poet show the importance of the hurricane? Think about:

- the development of her thoughts about the hurricane
- how the structure of the poem reflects her thoughts
- her use of language and imagery (see glossary, page 93).

Assessment objectives

In these activities you have:

- **developed interpretations of texts** e.g. explored how the hurricane makes the poet feel about living in England, and her roots
- **evaluated structural devices** e.g. how the argument of the poem is organized into stanzas.
- **evaluated linguistic devices** e.g. how the poet uses imagery

Nothing's Changed

Small round hard stones click
under my heels,
seeding grasses thrust
bearded seeds
5 into trouser cuffs, cans,
trodden on, crunch
in tall, purple-flowering,
amiable weeds.

District Six.
10 No board says it is:
but my feet know,
and my hands,
and the skin about my bones,
and the soft labouring of my lungs,
15 and the hot, white, inwards turning
anger of my eyes.

Brash with glass,
name flaring like a flag,
it squats
20 in the grass and weeds,
incipient Port Jackson trees:
new, up-market, haute cuisine,
guard at the gatepost,
whites only inn.

25 No sign says it is:
but we know where we belong.

I press my nose
to the clear panes, know,
before I see them, there will be
30 crushed ice white glass,
linen falls,
the single rose.

Down the road,
working man's cafe sells
35 bunny chows.
Take it with you, eat
it at a plastic table's top,
wipe your fingers on your jeans,
spit a little on the floor:
40 it's in the bone.

I back from the glass,
boy again,
leaving small mean O
of small, mean mouth.
45 Hands burn
for a stone, a bomb,
to shiver down the glass.
Nothing's changed.

Explanations

trouser cuffs: turn-ups
District Six: deprived but bustling area of Cape Town in
South Africa, home to 55,000 people, mainly coloured
Muslims. In 1966 the white ruling party ordered it to be
bulldozed as a slum and the community was destroyed.
Rebuilding was never completed
brash: offensively 'showy'
incipient: developing, just starting
haute cuisine: sophisticated, expensive cookery
bunny chows: a cheap and filling take-away food eaten
mainly by the poor

Exploring the poem

Tatamkhulu Afrika was born in Egypt in 1920 and now lives in South Africa. He began writing poetry when he was in his sixties and has now published four collections of poems about his experiences in South Africa. **Nothing's Changed** is from his third book, **Magabane**.

1. List all the details in the poem that tell you about the differences in the lives of black and white people in Cape Town.

2. What is it that makes the inn stand out and shows that it is a 'whites only inn'?

3. Seeing the inn takes the speaker back to his boyhood. What feelings does he recall from that period?

4. The poem's title and last line suggest that 'Nothing's Changed'. What things have not changed?

Structure

5. The poem is written in six stanzas (see glossary, page 95) of eight lines, but stanza four is split into two groups of 2 and 6 lines. Each stanza ends with a full stop.

   Why do you think stanza four breaks at line 24?

   Use a table like the one below to plot the development of ideas in each stanza of the poem.

Stanza	What is described	What the writer's feelings are	The details which show his feelings
Stanza 1	the run-down area the speaker is in	He seems quite neutral at this stage.	the word 'amiable' (line 8) used about the weeds
Stanza 2	his reaction to being in a particular area	An anger seems to build up in him.	the repetition leading up to the 'anger of my eyes' (line 16)
Stanza 3			

Language

6. Consider the poet's use of:
   - single-syllable words (see glossary, page 95)
   - alliteration (see glossary, page 93)   • onomatopoeia (see glossary, page 94)

   in stanza one. How do they help establish the mood of the poem?

7. How does the poet show the man's rising anger in stanza two?

8. Explain the effect of the following phrases in stanza three:
   - 'Brash with glass'   • 'flaring like a flag'   • 'it squats'.

9. The word 'glass' appears four times. Why is it an important word in this poem?

Culture

10. This is a poem about a divided society. On one side of the division there is a bulldozed township, bunny chows and plastic tables, while on the other there is a new hotel, *haute cuisine* and fine table-linen. What is the poet's attitude to this society? Give reasons for your answer.

Assessment objectives

In these activities you have:

- **developed interpretations of texts** e.g. explored the poet's feelings about racial injustice
- **evaluated structural devices** e.g. how the poet's feelings are developed in different stanzas
- **evaluated linguistic devices** e.g. the importance of the sounds of words.

Writing

1. In what ways can **Nothing's Changed** be seen as a hymn of protest? Do you think the unnamed man sees any hope for himself or others?

2. How effectively does the poem show the poet's feelings about the situation?

The poems together

Interpretation and culture

This **assessment objective** focuses on your ability to understand what the poems are about. The poems in this section have a distinctive voice related to many cultures and traditions. When writing about this across the poems:

- be aware of the individuality of each poem
- look at how the poems explore aspects and ideas of culture and tradition, and comment on similarities and differences.

Copy out a table like the one opposite to explore all the poems you study. Make notes in the boxes and add more columns if you wish to. Remember that examination questions may also link poems by

- use of language
- structure.

The activities on pages 84–5 provide an approach for writing about more than one poem.

Exploring the poems

Poem	Language	Roots	Caught between two cultures	Celebration	Protest	How things change
Search For My Tongue		Explores how your mother tongue is important				
Unrelated Incidents						
Half-Caste					Mocks those who cast a slur on people of mixed race	
Blessing						
Presents from my Aunts in Pakistan						
Ogun				Celebrates the traditional skills of his uncle		
Charlotte O'Neil's Song						
An Old Woman						
Hurricane Hits England						
Nothing's Changed					Protests about injustice and poverty – rich whites vs poor blacks	

Charlotte O'Neil's Song and Nothing's Changed

Charlotte O'Neil's Song and **Nothing's Changed** come from widely different cultures but display similar feelings and attitudes about oppression and injustice.

1   In **Charlotte O'Neil's Song**, how were the lives of mistress and servant different?

2   From whose point of view is the poem written? What feelings are associated with this point of view?

3   What is the poet's attitude? How is this made clear to the reader?

4   How are the lives of black and white people different in the world of **Nothing's Changed**?

5   From whose point of view is the poem written? What feelings are associated with this point of view?

6   What is the poet's attitude? How is this made clear to the reader?

Blessing and Ogun

You may be asked to write about two poems which have interested you and from which you have found out something about different cultures.

1   Which details in **Blessing** show what life is like in the place described?

2   Which details show the importance of water to the people in this place?

3   How is life in this place different from your own?

4   What has happened to traditional crafts in the country of **Ogun**?

5   What are the feelings of the poet's uncle towards the changes in his culture?

6   Although this poem is rooted in African culture, could its ideas apply to other cultures?

The same poems may be used in several different combinations. **Ogun**, for example, may also be considered alongside **An Old Woman**.

Ogun and An Old Woman

These two poems come from very different cultures but share the same idea, that it is people who should be valued in a society. The poems may be approached in the following way:

1   In **An Old Woman**, what details help to give a picture of the old woman and what her life is like?

2   In the first five stanzas, how does the narrator (see glossary, page 94) react to the old woman?

3   In lines 17–18 the old woman says something which completely changes the narrator's attitude to her. Describe the effect her words have. Why does the narrator respond to them so powerfully?

4   What does the last stanza tell us about the narrator's feelings about what has happened?

5   In **Ogun** what picture of the uncle is developed in the first 21 lines?

6   What can the uncle do that other people, 'the world', cannot?

7   What does the carved wooden figure tell us about the uncle's feelings about what has happened to him?

Presents from my Aunts in Pakistan and Hurricane Hits England

1 Explore the feelings of the two poets about living in England with their roots in another culture.

2 In **Presents from my Aunts in Pakistan** the girl says that she is 'half-English'. Which details in the poem emphasize her Englishness?

3 Which details in the poem show that she is still drawn to her Pakistani 'half' ?

4 What is her view of life in Pakistan? How are her aunts' lives different from her own?

5 Just as the arrival of presents in **Presents from my Aunts in Pakistan** affected the girl receiving them, the arrival of the hurricane in **Hurricane Hits England** affected the poet in this poem. Look at the first 26 lines and describe the ways in which she was affected by the storm.

6 Living in England, the poet feels she has become a 'frozen lake', her roots buried like those of the trees. The storm then comes and breaks the lake and uproots the trees. What does the last line of the poem tell you about how she feels now?

Search For My Tongue and Unrelated Incidents

1 In **Search For My Tongue**, what has caused the poet's mother tongue to 'rot'?

2 There are three different kinds of written language on the page. What does this show us about what it is like to have more than one language?

3 What does the extended metaphor (see glossary, page 93) of the opening bud tell us about the poet's attitude towards her 'mother tongue'?

4 In **Unrelated Incidents**, which aspects of the writing in this poem suggest that the poet is not someone from the BBC?

5 If the language of the poem is the 'trooth', what is the attitude of the poet towards 'BBC English'?

Language

You have already explored how the poets use language in the individual poems.

On these two pages you will look at how poets use language and how language varies or changes *across* the poems.

How language varies

Half-Caste and Search For My Tongue

Half-Caste is written in a variety of non-standard English while **Search For My Tongue** is written in two languages: standard English and Gujerati. The Gujerati is presented in its original form and also phonetically (see glossary, page 94).

1   What evidence is there to suggest that both of these poems are intended to be read aloud?

2   John Agard feels scornful towards people who use the expression 'half-caste'. How does the non-standard English of the poem give his feelings more force?

3   In **Search For My Tongue**, why do you think the writer provides a phonetic presentation of the Gujerati script in lines 17–30?

4   Comment on the connection between the ideas of the poems and the use of non-standard varieties of English in **Unrelated Incidents**, **Half-Caste** and **Search For My Tongue**.

Imagery

Hurricane Hits England and Blessing

In **Hurricane Hits England** and **Blessing** the poets use the real events of a violent storm and a burst pipe to develop a metaphor (see glossary, page 93) through which to explore ideas.

1   In **Hurricane Hits England**, what is the effect of comparing the storm with

- a 'howling ship'
- a person?

2   The real storm was accompanied by lightning. How does the poet use this as a metaphor to develop her ideas in the poem?

3   What is the effect of comparing the uprooted trees with 'whales' (line 23)? How does it connect with the idea of mystery?

4   In **Blessing** an apparently 'ordinary' thing like water is transformed by the poet's language into something of extraordinary significance. What is the effect of the suggestion of 'religious' imagery (see glossary, page 93) in the poem?

5   What does the phrase 'liquid sun' suggest to you?

6   What is the effect of the comparison of water with silver in line 9?

7   How have the writers of **Blessing** and **Hurricane Hits England** used language to give natural phenomena a greater significance?

Sounds

The rhymes (see glossary, page 95) in a poem like **Charlotte O'Neil's Song** should be explored in relation to the structure of the whole poem. Exploration of the language of a poem covers the poet's choice of words and sound using linguistic devices such as alliteration, consonance and assonance (see glossary, page 93). You could answer a question about the poet's language using an approach similar to the one below:

1   In **Ogun** the poet uses the sounds of words for different purposes. How does the writer use sound in line 4 and lines 15–16 to draw attention to his uncle's skills in transforming wood?

2   Find examples in lines 39–47 of alliteration, assonance and rhyme and examine their effect.

3   In **Nothing's Changed** the poet makes use of alliteration. Look at the repeated 'c' sound in 'click', 'cuffs, cans', 'crunch' in lines 1–6. What is the effect of the repeated sound?

4   Look carefully at lines 17–20. For what purposes does the poet use:
   • long and short vowel sounds   • alliteration?

Now find and comment on further examples of effective use of the sounds of words in these poems, for example, the use of 'sh' and 's' sounds in lines 7–11 of **Blessing** or the rhyming of 'clatter' and 'shatter' and 'crone' and 'alone' in lines 27–30 of **An Old Woman**.

Approaching a question on language

You may be asked a question which has language either as its main focus or as one of the bullet points. You should use the same approach in both cases, i.e. one which shows *how* the poets' use of language helps convey and develop their ideas.

Language as the focus of a question

1   Write about particularly effective use of language in **two** poems of your choice.

2   Choose **two** poems in which imagery is important and write about how the poets use images to convey their ideas.

3   Choose **two** poems and comment on how the poets use sound (alliteration, assonance, onomatopoeia) to describe people and places effectively.

4   Choose **two** poems written in different varieties of English and comment on the effectiveness of the language in each case.

Language as an important strand of a question

5   Choose **two** poems which present a view of culture which you find especially interesting. You should consider:
   • the poets' ideas
   • the way the poems are set out
   • the ways the poets use language.

Structure

Poems can be structured in many different ways. We can talk about a structure of ideas, where one idea follows another like the stages of a discussion or an argument.

Poems can have a structure of images, where one image seems to connect with another. Rhythm and rhyme (see glossary, page 95) are features which we usually associate with the structure of a poem, but not all poems have a regular metre (see glossary, page 94) and many of them do not rhyme.

Contrast can play an important part and so too can repetition. Structure is what gives a poem its organization, its shape and, sometimes, its sense of development. Dividing the poem into stanzas (see glossary, page 95) is one way to catch the eye and set the reader thinking, but poems can sometimes be organized in a less obvious way.

Stanza pattern

Search For My Tongue and Ogun

These poems are written in well-defined stanzas which help to show us the development of the poets' ideas.

1 **Search For My Tongue** is divided into three stanzas. How does this division help to show the development of an idea and a point of view?

2 The last nine stanzas of **Ogun** show us a change of mood and focus in the poem. How are the sentences organized in these stanzas and what is the effect of this?

Charlotte O'Neil's Song and Half-Caste

3 In **Charlotte O'Neil's Song**, how does the poet draw attention to:
   - the sheer number of tasks Charlotte had to do
   - her growing feelings about her mistress?

   How are the servant's feelings developed across the five stanzas of the poem?

4 Comment on the stanza pattern of **Half-Caste**. You might consider:
   - whether the five stanzas are five different stages of the poet's thought
   - the different lengths of the stanzas.

An Old Woman and Ogun

In these poems, the poets use stanza pattern and length to create a kind of turning-point in their poems.

5 How does the poet organize **Ogun** so that there are three clear areas of focus?

6 How does he emphasize the turning-point in the poem?

7 Which lines in **An Old Woman** mark the turning-point in the poem? Support your answers with evidence from the poem.

8 How do the different lengths of **Ogun** and **An Old Woman** influence your response to them?

Nothing's Changed and Presents from my Aunts in Pakistan

These two poems are very different in their shape and in the way the stanzas are organized.

9   What do you notice about the stanza lengths in each poem?

10   What other differences can you find?

11   To what extent do these differences match the different moods and subject matter of each poem? You could think about the titles of the poems and how these might have influenced the way the poets have chosen to organize them.

Rhythm and repetition

Charlotte O'Neil's Song, Hurricane Hits England and Half-Caste

Charlotte O'Neil's Song is the only poem in this section with an obvious and regular metre (see glossary, page 94), and this plays an important part in the development of its mood. Other poems create a kind of rhythm through their use of repetition.

1   Which words are repeated in **Hurricane Hits England** and what do they draw attention to?

2   **Half-Caste** makes use of a repeated question. What kind of question is being asked? Does it require an answer?

3   How does rhythm and repetition contribute to the different moods of each of these three poems?

Comparison and contrast

Search For My Tongue, Charlotte O'Neil's Song and Half-Caste

1   **Search For My Tongue** and **Charlotte O'Neil's Song** make powerful use of contrast and **Half-Caste** makes powerful use of comparison. Discuss the effect of contrast and comparison in these poems.

Line length

Unrelated Incidents and Half-Caste

1   **Unrelated Incidents** is organized in very short lines and is written with no stanza breaks. Why do you think the poet arranged it in this way?

2   **Half-Caste** is also written in quite short lines. What is the effect of this on the way you read the poem aloud?

Sample questions

When examiners write questions, they are giving you opportunities to meet specific **assessment objectives**. Before you answer any of the questions on this page, look at question 1 below and the model answer plan opposite.

In the examination, you have only 30 minutes in which to answer a question on the Poems from Other Cultures and Traditions. The model answer plan is structured in a way which helps you understand and address clearly the key assessment objectives on which the question is focused:

- interpretation
- language
- structure.

make cross-references	**1** Choose *two* poems which are about a person or about people. Write about:
develop and sustain an interpretation	• *the ideas and attitudes of the poets*
understand and evaluate structural devices	• *the ways the poems are set out*
understand and evaluate linguistic devices	• *the ways each poet uses language*
	• what the poems have to say about people's cultures.

2 Anger plays a central part in both **Ogun** and **Nothing's Changed**. Write about the ways the poets make this sense of anger clear to their readers.

3 **Presents from my Aunts in Pakistan** and **Search For My Tongue** both show people thinking about their 'roots'. How does each poem convey their thoughts and feelings?

4 **Half-Caste** and the poem taken from **Unrelated Incidents** are both written in varieties of non-standard English. What does this contribute to each poem? Write about:
- the point each poet is making
- the unusual use of language
- your response to each poem.

5 Choose **two** of your favourite poems from the ones you have studied. How do the poets explore different aspects of their culture?

6 How do **two** of the poets in this section explore the relationship between people and the places in which they live?

Model answer plan

Choose **two** poems which are about a person or about people. Write about:

- the ideas and attitudes of the poets
- the ways the poems are set out
- the ways each poet uses language
- what the poems have to say about people's cultures.

Plan	Examiner's observations
Ogun: Write about the uncle's skills. Show how the tone changes as the poet writes about cheap imports. The poet reveals his uncle's anger.	It's important to focus immediately on a key word in the question – 'people'. This section of your answer should consider the first bullet point about the ideas and attitude of the poet.
The poem is set out in several two-line stanzas which often run into each other. Rhyme is used for contrast as in the 'heavy' rhymes of lines 40–5 which contrast with the flow of lines 29–37.	The second bullet point is about structure. The point about contrast in use of rhyme should be linked to the contrasts in meaning in the poem.
Interesting use of imagery in lines 15–16, 23–24, 33. Some vivid description of the uncle and his workshop and in the picture of the forest.	The third bullet point. The emphasis here isn't on any imagery: you have to focus on imagery that is relevant to the presentation of the uncle. The forest imagery is relevant because it is used to reveal the poet's feelings about his uncle.
The poet is concerned about the loss of cultural identity, the attack on traditional skills.	Don't go too far in your response to this point. Knowledge about other cultures isn't an assessment objective.
Charlotte O'Neil's Song explores the human spirit – people standing up for themselves. We are shown how the lives of rich and poor were different before we see how the servant stood up for herself.	Don't feel you have to provide much of a link with the previous poem: comparison isn't necessary. Nor is it necessary to write things like 'This poem is written by Fiona Farrell' – in only 30 minutes you don't want to waste time on what is obvious.
There are four clear stages/stanzas. The poem has a strong rhythm and a lot of rhyme. Twenty-one of the 28 lines begin with 'I', 'You' or 'and': the first two draw attention to the conflict of the poem and the third shows how: **a** the hard tasks accumulated and **b** there were many freedoms in store for the servant.	As with the first poem it is important to try to relate your observations on the shape of the poem to the development of the poet's ideas. Pointing out that it is written in four stanzas won't on its own earn you any marks.
The language is fairly direct – no use of metaphor. The repetition of words like 'cleaned' suggests anger. Use of contrast in the sounds of words – as in 'silken pillow' (line 6) which may be contrasted with the blunt 'attic cot' (line 7).	In the limited time you have in the examination you can't adopt the same rigorous approach as in coursework: you need to be selective – choose some important features of the language. Don't feel you have to write about everything.
This poem shows anger with a culture which has exploited its poor, but rejoices in its basic freedom.	As with **Ogun** this would be a fairly brief response.

Preparing for the examination

The best preparation for the examination is to read and re-read the poems. The more you read them, the more you will see in them. Listen to what others have to say about them, but have the confidence to explore your own ideas.

Annotating the Anthology

For very good reasons you are only allowed to annotate your copy of the **NEAB English Anthology** lightly. Don't be tempted to put lots of notes in your copy. Examiners would far rather read your own response to a question about the poems than read an essay which is a collection of notes joined together. It is probably a good idea to make working copies of the poems which you can use to write on in class or at home when you are first looking at the poems. When you feel more comfortable with a poem you can then think about what light annotation will help you in the examination.

Organizing your time

It is very important to remember that you only have one hour for this part of the examination: thirty minutes for Poems from Other Cultures and Traditions, and thirty minutes for Poets in the English Literary Heritage. In this time you will need to:

- choose the question on Poems from Other Cultures and Traditions
- decide which poems you will base your answer on
- write your response.

You cannot write everything you know about the poems in only thirty minutes. It is important to bear that in mind. Examination questions are not designed to catch you out; they are written in a style which is intended to give you guidance on the kinds of things to write about. Read questions very carefully to see which aspects of the poems you should focus on.

Because you have to work quickly, it is important that you have an efficient approach:

- Highlight key words in the question and look carefully at bullet points. Bullet points are a guide from the examiners on what to write about.
- Choose poems which 'fit' the question – don't go into the examination having already made up your mind about which poems you are going to use.
- Even in such a short space of time, it is important to spend some time planning. Which poem will you look at first? What main points will you make?
- You will have to write about more than one poem. It can be helpful to write about one poem and then move on to the next as this makes planning easier.
- A key to improving your grades is learning how to develop a point. A paragraph, in most cases, will begin with a main point. The rest of the paragraph should add to that main point, explore it in further detail.
- Quotations are important to support the points you are making. They should follow each point. It is not good practice to begin with a quotation and then explain it. Avoid long quotations: a line or two, a phrase or even a word is sufficient.

Time spent planning your response in the examination will help you write a response that is clear. A well-organized, concise piece of writing in which you make focused and well-supported points is what examiners are looking for.

Glossary

alliteration: the repetition of initial letters in words next to, or near each other, to create a sound effect, for example: 'From pillar to post a pantomime' (page 12, line 5).

ambiguity: words and lines can sometimes suggest more than one interpretation, or meaning: poems are sometimes shaped so that their meaning is deliberately ambiguous, or uncertain, for example, **Blessing** (page 64) and **About His Person** (page 14).

antithesis: see **contrasting pairs**.

assonance: a delicate and subtle rhyme created by matching two or more accented vowels, for example 'played' and 'naked' (page 6), or identical consonants with different vowels, for example 'lost pain, lost iron' (page 72).

colloquial expressions: popular words and phrases which can be found in everyday conversation. This aspect of language is often linked to region, culture, historical period or occupation, for example: 'Pick a card, any card' (page 12) is a conjuring expression.

consonance: repetition of similar-sounding consonants in words or syllables, for example 'Hands burn/for a stone…' (page 80).

contrasting pairs: pairs of lines which draw attention to contradiction, disagreement, unfairness, or injustice. They are often used in speeches to persuade people of the rightness of an argument (see page 74). See also **pattern of three**.

couplets: pairs of lines which are often rhymed (see pages 12, 14, 74).

dialect: a particular version of a language with its own distinctive accent, grammar and vocabulary. Dialects are shaped by region and culture (see pages 60, 62).

imagery: the descriptive language used to create a particular picture, feeling, or mood in the reader's imagination.

metaphor: a particular kind of image, which describes something as though it were something else. In **Work and Play** (page 38) a swallow is described as 'a blue-dark knot of glittering voltage'. In **Ogun** (page 71) the carpenter's knuckles are described as 'silver knobs of nails'. A line like this works in two ways; it evokes the work-worn hands of the carpenter and the polished highlights of his skin, but it also suggests the nails which he hammers into the wood and the shine on them, created by the hammering. In an extended metaphor, the comparison is developed over the course of the poem (for example, the onion in **Valentine**, page 24 and the plant in **Search For My Tongue**, page 60).

metre: regularity of beat or rhythm in a poem can be established by stressing the same number of syllables in each line. In **Work and Play** (page 38), there are four stressed syllables to each line. The rhythm can be marked out by using / to mark a syllable that is stressed and ° for the syllables that are unstressed:

° / ° ° / ° ° / ° ° /

'With faces of torment, as space burns them blue'

About His Person (page 14) can be read to a regular beat, but the couplets alternate between eight stressed syllables (four to a line) and four stressed syllables (two to a line):

/ ° / ° ° / ° / °

'Five pounds fifty in change, exactly,'

° / ° /

'A postcard, stamped,'

mood: the atmosphere of a poem and the feelings which it evokes. Some of the sound patterns and images of **Ogun** (page 71), for example, evoke bitterness, energy and anger. The regular stanza lengths of **Nothing's Changed** (page 80) help to reinforce a mood of cold fury and conviction.

narrator: the speaker, the person who tells what happens in a poem or a story. The narrator's views and experiences *may* be those of the poet, but it would be a mistake to assume that this is always the case.

onomatopoeia: the sound of an onomatopoeic word helps to suggest what it describes or means, for example 'cracks' (see **Tractor**, pages 46, 47).

pattern of three: these are often used in speeches to persuade people of the rightness of an argument. They are usually constructed by giving three successive examples of something to drive a point home. Repetition of some of the same words in each example helps to create the pattern. See **Charlotte O'Neil's Song**, page 74:

'I scraped out your grate
and I washed your plate
and I scrubbed till my hands were raw.'

See also **contrasting pairs**.

personification: a type of metaphor where an animal, object or abstract idea is described as though it were human (see pages 48, 49 and pages 76, 77). This can help make what is being described 'come to life' but it can also be used to suggest how closely people and things might be related to each other. In **Hurricane Hits England** (page 78), the hurricane is personified as an old friend or relation from the poet's home country.

phonetic presentation: a way of spelling which matches letters to the sounds of words. The poem from **Unrelated Incidents** (page 62) uses phonetic presentation to represent the speaker's Glasgow accent.

puns: sometimes called a play on words, a pun is any word or expression which allows the poet to create more than one meaning. Puns can also be created by using words which have similar sounds but different meanings (see pages 12, 14, 16).

quatrain: a stanza or verse with four rhyming lines (see page 8).

rhyme: words that have a matching sound quality. Poems sometimes have rhyming words within the lines (**internal rhyme**) instead of, or as well as, at the end of them.

rhyme scheme: the pattern in which rhyming sounds occur within a poem. The first three stanzas of **The Warm and the Cold** (page 50) have a very definite rhyme scheme. In the first stanza, line 2 matches line 4; line 6 matches line 8 and line 10 matches line 12. This pattern is repeated in the next two stanzas.

rhythm: See **metre**.

simile: the direct comparison of one thing with another. For example, Moniza Alvi describes her traditional dress, a salwar kameez, as 'glistening like an orange split open' (page 68, line 4). Most similes make the comparison by using the words 'as' or 'like'.

sonnet: The sonnet form was developed in Italy in the fourteenth century. There are many variations of the form, but essentially, it has fourteen lines, a regular number of syllables to each line and a definite rhyme scheme. The English sonnet usually has ten syllables to the line and is organized into three quatrains and a concluding couplet. Sonnets are traditionally associated with love poetry, but they can be used to express other feelings and ideas (see **Poem**, page 8).

sound pattern: This is a general term which refers to any words or lines where sounds are repeated to create a mood, a feeling, or the noises of everyday life, for example: 'hit, hurt and flattened' (**Ogun**, pages 71–2 lines 6–7). In this line, repetition of the soft, consonant letters *h*, *f* and *t* combines with a succession of three short vowel sounds to suggest the quick, short, intakes of breath and the accompanying effort as the carpenter hammers the nails home. The effect can be realized by gentle exaggeration of the sound. See **War Photographer** (page 22, lines 21–2) for a good example of how sound patterns can be used to express a feeling, or a mood.

stanza: Poems are often organized into groups of lines called stanzas or verses. **Nothing's Changed** (page 80), for example, has regular, eight-line stanzas.

syllable: the basic sound unit of a word: 'flat' has one syllable; 'flattened' has two. **Poem** (page 8) is written with a very large number of single-syllable, or monosyllabic, words.

tone: the attitude of the poem, for example; serious, humorous, or sarcastic. The tone of **Half-Caste** (page 64) could be described as humorous and mischievous. The tone of a poem like the **untitled poem** by Simon Armitage (page 6) might be described as ambiguous.

voice: the voice of a poem helps to suggest its mood, attitude and purpose. Essentially, it can be defined as the way we might choose to express the words and lines, were we to read the poem out loud.

vowel sounds: the letters a, e, i, o, u are called vowels. The remaining letters of the alphabet are called consonants. It is difficult to define the 'length' of vowel sounds without taking into account the consonants placed next to them; if you are able to 'sing' or sustain a vowel sound, it is 'long', if the vowel sound allows you to speak it abruptly, it is 'short'.

Heinemann Educational Publishers
Halley Court, Jordan Hill, Oxford OX2 8EJ
A division of Reed Educational and Professional Publishing Ltd

OXFORD   MELBOURNE   AUCKLAND   JOHANNESBURG   BLANTYRE
GABORONE   IBADAN   PORTSMOUTH (NH) USA   CHICAGO

First published 1998

02 01 00
10 9 8 7 6 5

ISBN 0 435 10129 3

Designed and produced by 320 Design
Printed and bound in the UK by Bath Press

Acknowledgements

The authors and publishers would like to thank the following for permission to use copyright material:
Faber & Faber Ltd for 'I am very bothered...' p6, and 'Cataract Operation' p12, by Simon Armitage from
Book of Matches 1993; 'Poem' p8, and 'About His Person' p14, by Simon Armitage from *Kid* 1992; 'It Ain't
What You Do It's What It Does To You' p10, by Simon Armitage from *Zoom* Bloodaxe Books. Anvil Press
Poetry Ltd for 'War Photographer' p22, by Carol Ann Duffy from *Standing Female Nude* 1985; 'Valentine'
p24, and 'Before You Were Mine' p28, by Carol Ann Duffy from *Mean Time* 1993; 'Stealing' p26, by Carol
Ann Duffy from *Selling Manhattan* 1987; 'In Mrs Tilscher's Class' p30, by Carol Ann Duffy from *The Other
Country* 1990. Faber & Faber Ltd for 'Work and Play' p38, by Ted Hughes from *Season Songs*; 'The Warm
and the Cold' p42, 'Tractor' p46, 'Wind' p50, and 'Hawk Roosting' p52, by Ted Hughes from *Selected
Poems 1957–1981*. Carcanet Press Ltd for 'Search For My Tongue' p60, by Sujata Bhatt from *Brunizem*.
Random House UK Ltd for 'Unrelated Incidents' p62, by Tom Leonard from *Intimate Voices: Selected Works
1965–1983* Vintage 1995. Caroline Sheldon Literary Agency for 'Half-Caste' p64, by John Agard from *Get
Back Pimple* Viking Penguin 1996. Bloodaxe Books Ltd for 'Blessing' p66, by Imtiaz Dharker from *Postcards
from God* 1997. Oxford University Press for 'Presents from my Aunts in Pakistan' p68, by Moniza Alvi from
The Country at My Shoulder 1993, © Moniza Alvi 1993; 'Ogun' p71, by E. K. Brathwaite from *Islands* 1969,
© Edward Kamau Brathwaite 1969, reprinted in *The Arrivants* 1973. Auckland University Press for
'Charlotte O'Neil's Song' p74, by Fiona Farrell from *Cutting Out* 1987, © Fiona Farrell 1987. Curtis Brown
Ltd, London, on behalf of Grace Nichols for 'Hurricane Hits England' p78, from *Sunrise* Virago Press 1996,
© Copyright Grace Nichols 1996. Mayibuye Centre, University of the Western Cape, for 'Nothing's Changed'
p80, by Tatamkhulu Afrika.

The publishers have made every effort to trace the copyright holders, but if they have inadvertently
overlooked any, they will be pleased to make the necessary arrangements at the first opportunity.

The publishers would like to thank the following for permission to reproduce photographs on the pages
noted:

Jason Bell/Faber & Faber, p4; Superstock, pp6, 26; Magnum, pp8, 50; Format, p10; Tony Stone, p12;
Gareth Boden, p14; Penguin, pp20, 64; Corbis, pp21, 22, 28; Food Features, p24; Telegraph Colour Library,
p30; Carol Hughes/Faber & Faber, p36; Hulton Getty, pp38, 78; BBC Natural History Unit, p42; *Farmers
Weekly*, p46; NHPA, p52; Carcanet, p60; Random House, p62; © Succession Picasso/DACS 1998, p64;
Bloodaxe Books, p66; Oxford University Press, p68; Steve Butler, p74; Sheila Geraghty/Penguin, p78;
I-Africa, p80; Format, p60; ITN, p62; Panos, p66; Prodeepta Das, p69; Hutchison, p71; Mary Evans, p74;
Topham, p76; Daniel Laine/Corbis, p80.